OPPORTUNITIES EMERGING:
Social Change in a Complex World

bruce meder

Rainbow Juice Publishing • Coffs Harbour • 2017

Rainbow Juice Publishing
PO Box 6052
Coffs Harbour Plaza
NSW 2450
Australia
www.brucemeder.com

ISBN: 978-1-326-97368-1

First Printing: 2017

Cover art: Charlieaja | Dreamstime.com, used with permission

C.O.F.F.E.E. graphic p26, Rebekah Farr, used with permission

CONTENTS

	Dedication	vii
	Preface	ix
	Introduction	1
I	Emergency	3
II	Complex Context	7
III	Emergence	17
IV	A Quick (Caffeinated) Story	21
V	Coffee	25
VI	Creative	27
VII	Opportunities	55
VIII	Flow	63
IX	From	73
X	Encouraging	85
XI	Encounters	111
XII	The Whole Brew	149
	Acknowledgements	163
	About The Author	165
	Bibliography	167
	Index	173

For
Robin Anne Macgregor
(1957-2016)

PREFACE

I began writing this book more than 40 years ago, or at least it seems that way. The ideas that I have written about are ones that I played with, experimented with and evaluated through my work in community development, social justice groups, and with those around me. It took more than 40 years for these ideas to develop and for me to arrive at a point in my life where I feel confident and competent in writing them down in book form.

The acronym at the heart of this book (**C.O.F.F.E.E.**) came to me from an intuitive space but was provoked by the comments of a friend. Often when meeting someone for the first time in the company of a friend, Viv, I would inevitably be asked what I did. Before I could reply, Viv jumped in to answer, *"He just sits and has coffee all day."* Although I would contest this, there was an element of truth in her assertion. I did spend a lot of time sitting discussing things with people as part of my work. Often, admittedly, this was over a coffee. I found that I could work more effectively with people when the setting was informal than if we were seated in a formal, bureaucratic setting. Indeed, I often reflected that if I was sitting in my office then I was not doing my work properly. After a time I began to ponder Viv's blunt account of the nature of my work. One day, pondering what I did, with a cup of coffee in front of me, the **COFFEE** acronym was born.

What follows is a mixture of my experience, my research and reading, and my thinking. Into that mixture is thrown the wisdom of many people who I have been privileged to work alongside.

The people I most expect to read this book are those who in some ways want to change the world or at least a tiny corner of it. Perhaps you are fearful of the effects of climate change and have become disturbed by the endless outpourings of carbon emissions into our atmosphere. Perhaps you are concerned about the number of people attempting to escape the horrible destruction of war in their homelands. Maybe you are angry about the exploitation of peasant farmers in India or Africa and the uninformed way in which western consumers are complicit in that exploitation.

Maybe your concerns are closer to home. Perhaps you have witnessed or experienced the horrors of domestic violence and want to ease the burden of victims or find ways to stop the endless cycle of abuse. Perhaps you are concerned that your children have nowhere to play and that businesses and huge corporations are encroaching upon playgrounds and open spaces in your neighbourhood. Maybe you want to bring back the neighbourliness and friendliness that has been exorcised from your local community.

Perhaps your concerns are for the non-human species living on our planet. Perhaps you want to save the orangutans, whales or tigers from extinction, or help preserve a patch of native bush that is the habitat of many species of insects, birds and fish.

Whatever your concerns, you will find that there are others who share them. There will also be those with contrary concerns, perhaps even antagonistic. How do you go about resolving these concerns? How do you work with those who agree with you? Importantly too, how do you work with those who disagree with you? How do you obtain answers when you don't even know the right questions to ask?

This book may help you.

The book begins with an exploration the ideas of complexity and emergence in Chapters 1 to 4. In these chapters I have tried to provide a context for what is to follow in the rest of the book. I have attempted to make accessible the, sometimes mysterious, ideas of Complexity Theory, Chaos Theory and Emergence. These ideas have a bearing on the overlapping concerns that we have for the world, yet sometimes it is difficult to figure out how they impact our social world. Those working in social change, community development and/or sustainability may intuitively understand this new paradigm, but may not have a fully developed contextual framework to work within. This small text is an attempt by one writer to contribute towards that framework. I hope that I have managed to make the understanding of the paradigm a little easier.

Chapters 5-11 present a way of thinking with which to approach the way in which we act upon the world. Each chapter delves into and explains the individual words that make up the **COFFEE** acronym, i.e. **C**reative **O**pportunities **F**low **F**rom **E**ncouraging **E**ncounters. The final chapter (12) then pieces it all together. For those readers who want to get straight to the "how to" aspects then you may like to skip the first four chapters and head directly to chapter 5. A word of caution though. These chapters are not a "how to" section; it is more a way of thinking, an approach style if you like. It does not say; "do this, then follow it with that." It suggests that the way in which we think about our analysis, problem-solving and decision-making is just as important as the practical strategies we may employ. Additionally, the ideas developed in chapters 5-11 follow directly from an understanding of complexity, chaos and emergence. Hence, I would suggest not skipping chapters 1-4 as they do provide the basic context within which the **COFFEE** of the remainder of the book is brewed.

Finally, a few words about words. I have struggled with how to describe the people who are likely to read this book. A few paragraphs ago I referred to you as those who "want to change the world." Many phrases have been used for those of us who want to change the world over the years. Free-thinker, revolutionary, agitator, change activist/agent, or rebel have all been used at one time or another. Some have used these labels to dismiss or condemn. Others have accepted them with pride. All of them, in the end, are simply labels. However, I still needed a word or phrase that could be used to signify those who "want to change the world." Initially, I thought that I would use the term social change activist. However, that phrase is insufficient when we think of the concept of emergence presented in this book. The phrase tends to suggest a definitive approach with pre-determined outcomes. However, as this book will explain, the world cannot be viewed in such deterministic fashion.

I was drawn to Shakespeare's assertion in *As You Like It* that *"All the world's a stage/And all the men and women merely players."* This thought allowed me to identify that we are actors and creators at the same time, yet our roles are only part of the whole and that even the stage on which we act is only part of an even bigger auditorium. I have come to refer to people who want to change the world as *activators* (combining *activist* with *creator*). Hopefully, this more explicitly recognises the interconnections between all of us; and that we create our world together. Indeed, the idea of creation suggests that our journey/play/drama is never finished, and we never know whereabouts our journey may take us. Our play remains unfinished.

I hope that you enjoy reading this and find within the complexity a simplicity that resonates with your own experience and wisdom.

Coffs Harbour
March 2017

INTRODUCTION

Everywhere we look there are emergencies. Globally those emergencies go under various guises: climate change, war, terrorism, refugee crises. Nationally we face emergencies of depression and anxiety, drug use, unemployment. In our local communities we see emergencies when we look around and see homeless people, domestic violence, youth disenchantment, racism, traffic congestion. Often too, we hear these emergencies around our own dinner table or in our living rooms: fathers who cannot connect with their teenage sons and daughters, teenagers who think that their parents are ignorant dinosaurs, the husband and wife who have drifted apart emotionally and now just exist side by side in a loveless zone. No matter whether our telescope or microscope is focused on the whole planet, or whether it zooms into our local neighbourhood we see emergencies.

We see these emergencies plain as day. We know what's wrong with the world and our street, don't we? We want to fix it. We analyse, we plan, we act. What happens? Nothing changes – the emergencies are still there. Then, we either burn out through continually "beating our heads against brick walls," or we become disillusioned and give up.

Maybe instead of thinking in terms of emergency, we need to think in terms of emergence.

Emergence is an aspect of Chaos Theory and Complexity Theory. The early chapters of this book will outline and describe each of these three mechanisms – emergence, chaos, complexity.

Once we understand the way in which these mechanisms work it becomes apparent that emergence leads us to realise that nothing is predictable. We cannot plan for the future nor predict what will happen when we act with any certainty. Chaos is inherently unpredictable.

But, we want something better, don't we? We want a better world, or at least, a better street or household. If nothing is predictable, then how do we act?

The remainder of this book seeks to answer that by suggesting that we do not need to plan in any deliberate, mechanistic, linear fashion. What we need to do is be on the alert for creative opportunities that flow from the encouraging encounters that we have each and every day. In fact, this simple idea can be summarised in a simple acronym:

Creative **O**pportunities **F**low **F**rom **E**ncouraging **E**ncounters©

That's right – **COFFEE**. The act of having a coffee together brings to mind both the acronym and the simple act of meeting someone to share stories, ideas, thoughts, and opportunities. Chapters 6-11 of this book take each of the words in the acronym as the title of a chapter and explores in more depth that particular aspect of the acronym. Following that the acronym is considered in its entirety, i.e. as a unified idea, not the sum of its parts, but, well … the emergent whole.

The acronym has the advantage of being easy to remember, as well as indicating a very simple approach to emergent change. There is nothing really complicated about it, nothing esoteric, nothing that you need to go off and undertake a University degree in. It is very, very simple. Therein lies the seeming irony: the emergencies are complex, yet the way we face them and tackle them is not complex – it is simple.

So, go make yourself a cup of coffee and read on.

I
EMERGENCY

How many of us worry about the state of the world? When we read the latest Intergovernmental Panel on Climate Change (IPCC) report we get worried. When we read of thousands of refugees fleeing across the borders of Afghanistan, Syria, or Somalia and into Europe, we get worried. When we turn on the television and watch paramedics struggling to contain Ebola in western Africa we get worried. When we hear Prime Ministers speak of "imminent terrorist threats" or watch the violence erupt in Iraq, Syria, the Gaza Strip or Ukraine, we get worried.

Closer to home, we read daily newspapers reporting on the growth in youth suicide, the obesity problem or the increase in rates of depression and anxiety disorders. These reports are worrying.

We don't have to dig very far to notice that the amount of plastic in our landfills and our oceans is growing rapidly or that e-waste is now a concern. All worrying.

We look around our own neighbourhoods and communities. We see people living off the street, we see young men sitting outside the Courthouse on Monday mornings waiting for the bailiff to call them before the judge. We see elderly people, or people with disability, struggling to cope with the kerbing or the steps into buildings. If we think of what it is like for all these people, we get worried.

We look to our leaders; the Prime Ministers, Presidents and Premiers of nations. We watch as they debate the issues at Climate Change Summits, G20 meetings or within our own parliaments, senates and congresses. In our own cities and towns, we watch and listen to our mayors and councillors debating and deliberating in Town Halls and council chambers.

Then we really do get worried, because we realise that very few of our leaders have any idea of how to avert these emergencies or, worse still, have no interest in doing so. Many times we may even wonder if they are contributing towards the emergencies - grinning like the pale rider of death, racing full tilt towards the apocalyptic abyss (see box).

Now we have another emergency to add to the growing list: our public decision-making institutions and bodies, or what we otherwise know as government. Democracy (or at least we call it that) is in a state of emergency. We don't trust politicians, we are wary of the lobbying power of powerful, rich corporations; we are withdrawing from political processes by not voting and joining traditional political parties in fewer and fewer numbers.

In fact, with all the ills of the world only apparently getting worse and no-one seeming to care, it looks as if the world and we humans along with it are on the brink of a series of serious emergencies.

Is this our fate? To collapse from a multi-faceted emergency? Is there an alternative? Perhaps there is.

Instead of **EMERGENCY** we might look towards **EMERGENCE**.

Emergence is an aspect of chaos and complexity theory. Although these theories arose within the mathematical and scientific arenas, they have useful insights for those working for social justice, community development and/or sustainability.

Before explaining what emergence is, I need to take a short tour of the hitherto prevailing western-styled world-view.

The Historical Western World-View

For centuries we have lived in and looked at the world. We have tried to explain it and then, particularly in the western tradition, tried to manipulate it for our own purposes. We have tried to explain it largely by breaking it down into smaller and smaller pieces, into its component parts. So, in the sciences, we have studied atoms, DNA or mitochondria.

We have tried to discover how the world works by assuming a linear cause and effect dynamic. If A happens then B follows and always does so. Much of our basic scientific knowledge is based on this: Newton's Laws are a classic example.

Once we could explain the world and understand how it worked, we then tried to manipulate it by planning and predicting what would happen because of our plans.

Then we become amazed or confused, even frustrated, that things don't go according to plan. This is true in the scientific world and even truer in the world of human agency.

So, why doesn't it happen the way we plan and predict? After all, we understand what makes up the world and we know how it works, don't we?

Chaos, complexity and emergence help us to look at the world in a different way: a way that presents us with a radically different world-view, a new paradigm. With this different world-view, it may be possible to avert the multi-faceted emergency facing us.[1] What's more, we may be able to do so collectively, without the need to put our faith in our current leaders.

---

[1] Mind you, as we shall see, we might not be able to.

II
COMPLEX CONTEXT

If you read anything today relating to social change or community development there will often be a reference to society, humanity or the world being a complex place. Complexity is the catch-phrase of the age. "We live in a world of complexity," "the new order is complex," "the issues facing communities (or society) are complex." What do we mean by this? What does it mean to say that the world is complex? How are the issues of today complex?

The word "complexity" is not just a throw-away word used to label something or a situation we don't fully understand. Complexity has a theoretical basis in scientific circles where its full term is "complex systems theory," (also known as Complexity theory). Complexity theory began to emerge in the early part of the twentieth century when scientists (particularly physicists) began to realise that the western linear explanation of the world was not fulfilling the promise of scientific understanding. Western science, beginning with the Enlightenment in the 17th Century had built its understanding of the way in which the world worked upon a foundation of order. This order was open to experimentation that would lead to a complete understanding of cause and effect.

It wasn't long before the ideas of cause and effect, order and events proceeding along predictable paths, entered the thinking of politics, philosophy and eventually everyday life. Science could understand the whole by breaking it down into smaller and smaller parts. Science became biology, chemistry, and physics. Biology became zoology, ecology, entomology, etc. Chemistry became biochemistry, neurochemistry, etc. And physics became mechanics, dynamics and quantum physics. Further and further specialisation – more and more known about less and less.

In society we followed in science's footsteps. Life was broken down into its component pieces. We had boxes and compartments for work, play, social life, spirituality, family time, consuming. In politics, the issues that we contended with were handed over to portfolios in housing, energy, transport, health, education, foreign affairs, immigration, defence, social welfare, ad nauseam.

That was how we understood the ways of the world and ourselves. That was the way in which we approached the world.

But then it all went pear-shaped. Quantum physics discovered that everything was not as it seemed – Einstein referred to some of this as "spooky action." Biology discovered that eco-systems survived if there was diversity and tended to collapse if even just one part of that eco-system was removed (see box). The insight that hammered the final nail in the coffin of order came in meteorology where it was found that even the tiniest difference in initial conditions could have a major, significant impact on the outcome, so much so that the outcome was no longer entirely predictable.

In 1961 Edward Lorenz (a meteorologist) was working on a computer model of weather patterns. He had already run one computer simulation which had taken hours. Wishing to repeat the

> **Eco-system Diversity and Collapse**
> The removal of wolves from Yellowstone National Park is a well-documented case in point. Wolves began to be eradicated in the Park in the 1920s because of a perceived danger to humans. In the late 1990s researchers pondered the question: "why are the aspen trees dying?" They came to realise that the removal of wolves allowed the elk to flourish. Aspen seedlings are a favoured food of browsing elk and so the growth in numbers of elk was having a devastating effect on the regeneration of aspen trees. In turn, the lack of trees affected the beavers that used the trees to build their dams and homes. The loss of trees, and lack of the dams that beavers built with them, contributed to greater soil erosion. The whole eco-system was deteriorating. Since wolves have been reintroduced to Yellowstone National Park ecologists have found that the natural eco-system is beginning to restore itself.

simulation, but not wanting to have the computer run for such a length of time, he fed in the numbers from part way through the simulation and then left it to complete the programme. He went to get a cup of coffee. (Remember this was in the days before fast computers. It had a capacity of just 4 kW and cost $47,000 – in the late 1950s! Little wonder he had time to go for a coffee.) When he came back he was amazed. The final configuration of this second run bore absolutely no resemblance to the first run. What was going on?

When Lorenz looked carefully at the data he found that when he loaded the numbers the second time he had inputted the data to three decimal places (as this was what was printed out by the computer printer.) However, the computer used six decimal places in its computations and had rounded those six places to the three places that Lorenz inputted. Lorenz had assumed that the "insignificant" difference between six decimal places and three would make no significant difference to the final result. He was wrong. What Lorenz had discovered later became known as the "Butterfly Effect."

Briefly, the "Butterfly Effect" is a metaphor used to describe how a seemingly insignificant event can trigger major outcomes. The metaphor says that when a butterfly flutters its wings over the Amazon jungle this can trigger a thunderstorm over Tokyo. Intuitively we know how this happens, we have experienced it. How many readers have set out from their homes to go somewhere then realised that you have left your keys or wallet or some other item in the house? You stop for only a few seconds to retrieve the item and then continue on. You get in your car and start driving to where you are going. You end up in a traffic jam that a few seconds before wasn't there, or you miss being in a road accident by those few seconds. Maybe you arrive slightly late and miss the elevator and have to wait for the next one and end up meeting someone who becomes a life-long friend. Those few seconds led to quite different events in your life than would have happened had you not left your keys or wallet behind.

This "sensitivity to initial conditions" is one aspect of a complex system. Complex systems are characterised also by:

- The number of parts of the system and relationships between them being large enough to effectively be non-trivial.[2]
- Feedback playing a part in how the system reacts to inputs and outputs. Thus, it is possible for a system to react differently to an input at one time than it did at an earlier time. You could say that the system has learnt from the earlier experience and has adapted in response.
- It is adaptive; adapting to its environment and in turn the environment adapting to it.

With respect to the systems that social change agents and community development workers are working in it is obvious that the systems are far from trivial. Community development works with groups of people (neighbourhoods, suburbs, societies etc.) often numbering in the hundreds or thousands.

Anyone who has worked in communities for some time knows that there are forces acting from outside a community that impact either positively or negatively upon the community to varying degrees. Similarly, a community development worker will have seen how one sector within a community may influence another sector and that this may in turn influence another. Furthermore, the amount or intensity of these influences will vary and fluctuate over time. These phenomena are examples of feedback at work on the "community system."

The last of the characteristics of complex systems is obvious when one considers that communities are always in flux, ever shifting. Residents come and go, some remaining in the same geographical community all their lives, others remaining for only a matter of months or even weeks before moving on to another place. Even within "communities of interest" the membership will fluctuate. With such fluctuation comes adaptation. A stalwart of a community is

---

[2] A non-trivial situation is one in which the number of parts and/or the relationships between them are not immediately or clearly obvious.

often sorely missed when they move, as the community then has to find another way of providing the benefit that that resident brought to the community.

Before proceeding, it is worth noting that complexity is not another way of saying complicated. Complexity refers to the inter-relationships between parts of a system, whereas complicated suggests that the system has many parts. Thus, it is possible for a system to be both non-complicated (simple) and yet complex at the same time. In a simple system, it is relatively straightforward enough to work out the number of parts (or stakeholders or players etc.). In a complex system, however, even if it is possible to determine all the key stakeholders, it may be impossible to gain a complete understanding of the various inter-relationships between them.[3] This idea – that of complexity and simplicity co-existing – is one that we will come back to, as it has relevance to how our **COFFEE** approach works.

But the world isn't just complex, it is becoming increasingly so according to many commentators. What is driving that increase in complexity? Consider these five trends over the past half-century or so.

Travel

In the early half of the 20th century most people travelled from one side of the world to the other by ship. Australians and New Zealanders travelling overseas to Europe on their OE[4] often did so by

---

[3] An example may help clarify this. Suppose you know exactly how many people make up a particular group. Let's say it is a dozen. This is not complicated. There are 12 people, you can name them all, discover their ages, measure their heights and weights etc. But, try to work out the relationships between those people. There will be relationships between any pair, which will be different if a third person is added, and different again if you take 5, 6, 7 or a different number of them. The mathematics produces a total of well over 3,000 different combinations of relationships possible. When you consider that those relationships will change over time, it is easy to see how this can be very complex, even though the number of people (just 12) is far from complicated.

[4] OE = Overseas Experience. A common shorthand used by young people in Australia and New Zealand to describe their desire to travel to overseas destinations in their late teens and early twenties.

boarding an ocean liner and spending the next few weeks travelling via the Panama or Suez Canal to European ports. The second half of the century saw airfares reduce drastically and more airline routes opened up. This transformed the nature of travel. Within a decade or so, the time taken to get from one side of the world to the other reduced from a week or two to around a day.

Even within nations travel has sped up significantly. Cars are much quicker, break down less often, are comparatively cheaper and roads are better constructed. All of this adds up to private vehicle ownership rising and hence travel within nations becoming easier.[5] In less than a century western societies have become highly mobile. Public transport too has contributed to the ease with which people move about.

Faster, more frequent and easier travel has meant that people come and go between communities more rapidly than they did only fifty or sixty years ago.

Communication

When did you last post a letter? For most readers, it is unlikely that it was within the last week and quite possibly not within the last couple of months, maybe not even in the last few years. The rise of the Internet, emails, texting, iPhones and other mechanisms has provided us with virtually immediate communication with anyone on the planet. With technologies such as Facebook, Twitter and the like, it is possible to befriend people that you have never even met, and may even know nothing about.

Communication has sped up even faster than has our travel. A letter from Australia to England would have taken around a week or more in the early to mid-twentieth century – about the same time as it took to travel the same route. Today, travel from one side of the

---

[5] The total number of cars in the world has recently begun to reduce, having risen from less than 90 million in 1970 to almost 140 million in 2008. The number of kilometres travelled per vehicle per year, however, has continued to climb, to over 20,000 km in 2013. Source: *Transportation Energy Data Book, edition 35,* October 2016.

planet to the other will take up to 24 hours, but it is possible to communicate within seconds. Sounds more complex, doesn't it?

Information

Think too, of the amount of information that exists. In 2007 there were 6,580 daily newspapers in the World. Almost 800,000 new books are published each year.[6] Even if you were able to read one book a day, just to get through one year's worth of books would take almost 30 lifetimes. Even keeping up with the daily newspapers is beyond one person's ability. Then there are scientific papers and articles. By the beginning of the 21st Century, almost 700,000 were being published per year, an increase of 300,000 in just 20 years.[7] And that's just the printed medium. Research from UCLA notes that we are subjected to the equivalent of around 170 or more newspapers each day, more than five times the amount we were bombarded with in the mid-1990s.

The virtual medium, via the Internet, is even more information rich. Between 1995 and the middle of 2011 the number of registered domains on the Internet rose from a modest 15,000 to a staggering 350 million with 150,000 new URLs registered each day.

Technology

Our use of technology has risen immensely since the end of World War II. Some of it has already been alluded to in the previous two examples. Think of television. Although it had been technically available in the 1920s, it wasn't until after the end of WW II that black and white television started to become widespread. By the 1970s black and white television had largely given way to colour. The number of television channels proliferated and today it is possible to not just subscribe to television channels, but also to use the television to play DVDs, Blue-Ray or use as a computer monitor. Since the beginning of the 21st century, movies, documentaries, news,

---

[6] Google calculates that the total number of books ever written to be 130 million.

[7] This figure is that for natural sciences and engineering.

game shows and other genres have become available on hand-held phones. Ironically, we now are more likely to watch "television" on a tiny screen that rests in the palm of our hand, or, at the other extreme, on large-screen Plasma TVs.

Technology has bloomed since the 1950s. All of the following have been invented since then: microwave oven, cardiac pacemaker, communication satellites, smoke detector, digital music, hydrogen bomb, the Internet, the PC, CDs, MP3 players, hovercraft, GPS, laser, barcode, Kevlar, ATMs, roller blades, cell phones, Prozac, hepatitis B vaccine, hybrid cars. Most of these are day-to-day items (okay, maybe not the H-bomb) that seem to have been with us forever.

In 1970 Alvin Toffler published *Future Shock* in which he described the process by which the rate of change within society was having a debilitating psychological impact on individuals and whole societies. He coined the term *information overload* to describe this. According to Toffler, the overall production (and consumption) of goods and services doubles every 50 years. Who could argue that his basic tenet is incorrect?

Financial Systems

Once upon a time we traded items for other items, often by a simple swap. Money was invented approximately 5,000 years ago. Shares were first introduced around 800 years ago and then derivatives, with the Japanese being credited with establishing the first exchange in the 17th century. It wasn't until 1973 that the first modern options market began, with the opening of the Chicago Board Options Exchange (CBOE).

In the years since the opening of the CBOE, the range and variety of financial systems and financial trading mechanisms have rapidly expanded. Today it is possible to trade in stocks and shares (which most people will have heard of) and also in commodities (coffee, oil, cotton and even pork bellies), or currency (via the FOREX market). If you want to trade, you can be a long-term investor, a speculator, a day-trader or a scalper. You can take the long side or the short side. You can be a technical analyst and use charts to make your decisions, or you can be a fundamental analyst using your knowledge of the company itself. You might want to use stochastics, candlesticks or Elliot Waves to help you, or perhaps the Black-Scholes Equation. If you like, you can trade in derivatives (warrants, options, futures, e-minis and on and on).

The financial world is a vast, interconnected and (for the unwary) scary place. In short, it is complex.

As if each of these examples of increased complexity isn't enough, the connections between them only add to the complexity. Financial trading has capitalised on the advance in technology and rapid communication means that trading can take place almost instantaneously. The range and speed of travel mean that goods can be shifted around the world much faster than previously, allowing for consumers to partake of goods and services from all over the world. These complexities have their benefits as well as their problems. Irrespective of whether you think globalisation is beneficial or harmful, it cannot be disputed that the world is more complex because of it and becoming increasingly so.

Yes, it may be becoming more and more complex, but we need not despair. Out of Complexity Theory, the concept of Emergence has arisen, which gives us a possible route out of any despair and can also lead us away from the coming emergencies.

III
EMERGENCE

Emergence – what's emergence? Let's begin with a simple example that illustrates some of the features of emergence.

Everyone has heard of the elements hydrogen (H, oxygen (O and carbon (C). What do we know about each of them? We know that hydrogen is bitter, sour smelling, <u>and</u> explosive. We know that oxygen is tasteless, odourless and a vital ingredient of the air that we breathe. We know that carbon is also tasteless, inert, and cold.

Now, what would we expect to get if we combined these three elements like this: C_2H_5OH? (Those of you who understand chemistry, please put aside your acquired knowledge for the time being and assume that all you know is the properties of each individual element as outlined above). From our knowledge of each of hydrogen, oxygen and carbon we may expect to get a compound that is largely tasteless, perhaps slightly bitter, with a very faint smell. Knowing what we know about hydrogen we may want to be wary of the compound – it could be explosive.

But, what do we get? We get ethanol – an alcohol that most of us associate with wine, beer or spirits. The result of this particular mixture of hydrogen, oxygen and carbon is unexpected and unable to be explained by our knowledge of the individual elements. That's emergence.

Emergence is a coherent structure or property that arises from the organisation of component parts where the emergent structure or property cannot be predicted from knowledge of the individual component parts.

As well as being unpredictable, other features of emergence are that:

- It creates an order out of disorder,

- It is sensitive to initial conditions. Meaning that very small changes in the initial state can produce massively different outcomes. (Often known as the *Butterfly Effect* discussed in the previous section),
- It is often spontaneous,
- It is not simply the sum of its parts,
- It is often dynamic and continuously evolving,
- It is a bottom-up process, not a top-down one. The process is an emergent one rather than one that is compelled.

A couple of examples of emergence may help to make the process understandable. One example is local and personal to me, the other is global.

In February 2011 I was living in Redcliffs, a beachside suburb in Christchurch, in the South Island of New Zealand. At 12.51 pm on the 22nd of February a magnitude 6.3 earthquake hit the city. 185 people were killed – three of them personal friends. Lives were lost, buildings collapsed, properties destroyed, people were traumatised, infrastructure was damaged. Less than 600 metres from my home, some houses were crushed under boulders fallen from the cliffs above. Meanwhile, above them, other houses hung off the side of cliffs that had collapsed. Thousands of families were without power and water for weeks.

But that is not the focus here; the focus is on what happened afterwards.

Within minutes of the earthquake hitting, neighbours were helping neighbours; strangers were asking one another if they were alright. People in suits and city clothes were pulling at fallen building materials desperately attempting to save those trapped inside collapsed buildings. In the suburbs people were checking on the elderly or comforting distressed children.

The day after the earthquake, a makeshift tent using a tarpaulin was strung up in the tiny shopping centre of Redcliffs offering local residents information (that was difficult to get), food, advice or just someone to talk with. Later, a local resident donated his small caravan to the "information and support centre." This caravan housed a computer, a mobile phone and somewhere to store stuff. The centre was staffed entirely by volunteers.

Water was trucked in by farmers from the countryside. A group of women in the North Island baked cake and sent it down. One young man turned up in his ute from Nelson (a 5-hour drive away), approached us at the centre and said: "I'm a builder, how can I help?" Another young man who was a plumber arrived from the very south of the island offering similar assistance. A Student Volunteer Army from the local University mobilised to help shovel liquefaction.[8]

The point of all this is that none of it was organised or facilitated by an official, central, or government body. It emerged spontaneously. The parts were all there: the tarpaulin, the caravan, the water, the builder, the plumber and their tools, the people. But none of them separately could explain what emerged to cope with the disaster. Indeed, officialdom responded slowly – one suburb was still without portaloos weeks after the earthquake.

This is not a criticism of officialdom, rather it is a recognition that the way in which humans mostly respond to adversity or tragedy is with spontaneity, with immediate compassion, and they do so without having to be directed, organised or planned. This is emergence.

The second example is a well-known global one.

On 25 January 2011 over 50,000 people occupied Tahrir Square in Cairo. By the end of the month the number had grown to over 300,000. The Arab Spring was well underway, with calls for major reform and democracy throughout that part of the world. This massive movement began with a simple video message on Facebook

---

[8] Liquefaction is the uprising of liquefied soil and sand. Prior to the earthquakes Cantabrians had hardly heard of the word. Within days the word "liquefaction" and the word "munted" (meaning destroyed) became two of the most often used words in the city.

by a young Egyptian woman. The video went viral "and the rest is history" (as it's said).[9]

The Arab Spring went on to inspire one of the largest global demonstrations in favour of equity, democracy, and sustainability that the world has seen – the Occupy Movement. Zuccotti Park in New York was occupied from 17 September 2011 and similar occupations spread quickly throughout the world. Within a month, protests were organised in over 80 countries.

Did anyone predict this? Did anyone plan this? No – it emerged.

So then, the world often evolves through the process of emergence. The question now becomes: if emergence is unpredictable, spontaneous, sensitive to initial conditions and is a bottom-up process, how can we create the space in which the outcomes that we want are more likely to emerge?

I like to think that we have a cup of coffee. Not just any coffee though – there are many cafés and coffee sellers offering environmentally friendly and socially just coffee. Amongst these are the certifications of *Fair Trade* or *Rainforest Alliance*.[10] Check out with your local café and insist on coffee that does not exploit the local farmers or the environment.

---

[9] This is an excellent example of the Butterfly Effect: a very small input (a Facebook posting by one person) having an enormous outcome (50,000 people growing to hundreds of thousands over the next few months and eventually to becoming a world-wide movement).

[10] *Fair Trade* is a certification that the product provides better prices, decent working conditions, local sustainability and fair terms of trade for farmers and workers in the developing world. The *Rainforest Alliance Certified™* seal is an internationally recognised symbol of environmental, social and economic sustainability that helps both businesses and consumers do their part to ensure a brighter future for us all.

IV
A QUICK (CAFFEINATED) STORY

Soon after I began work in 1994 as a Community Development Adviser for the Christchurch City Council in the northern part of the city, I met and introduced myself to a number of community organisations. I met the staff and management personnel of numerous groups, including youth organisations. In the Papanui area, there were three or four actively engaged youth groups plus a community-based Alternative Education School that catered for secondary-aged students who otherwise did not fit into mainstream education. We met in church halls, cluttered offices, or at one of the cafés in the local shopping mall, often over a cup of coffee.

As we talked, one of the themes that came up time after time was that all these youth groups were very involved with the youth they worked with, but were uncertain as to what the other groups were doing and that there was little, if any, coordination between them. None of them had the time to spend facilitating coordination; they were so focused and intent on the programs and activities they were running for the young people in their own groups. This was not through lack of interest or not recognising the worth of such coordination. Most funders do not provide funding to community organisations in order for the organisation to help coordinate things between them and other organisations. The outcomes they are funded for are very much targeted towards the programs they run. Eventually, it dawned on me that this role was one that I could, and should, fulfil. After all, I was paid to facilitate community development in the area. One of the best ways to do that is to work with what already exists and to build the capacity to respond. The capacity was already there, what was lacking was the space (physical and temporal) for these groups to network and coordinate.

A meeting of youth workers from the various groups was brought together and met in the Board Room of the City Council Service Centre in Papanui. I facilitated the meetings and another staff member acted as note-taker. As we talked, we learnt about the differing foci of each of the groups, their desires and their strengths. After meeting every couple of months for a year or so, someone in the group mentioned that most of us in the room were adults, and although we worked with youth and had the interests of youth at heart, we were not young people. If the network of youth groups was going to have any positive benefit for young people then we needed to involve young people, we needed to recognise and understand their needs and desires.

We decided to bring young people together for a day to workshop over various youth issues and to have a bit of fun at the same time. The Great North-West Youth Summit was born. In just a few weeks the summit went from an idea to reality. More than 400 young people turned up from six or seven high schools and many youth groups in the north-west part of Christchurch. Workshops on health, safety, well-being, recreation, training, dealing with authority, family, sexuality and other topics were spread throughout the day-long summit. Interspersed between these workshops was free music by local youth bands plus other forms of entertainment.

One workshop looked at the issue of a youth space. In the Papanui area, young people identified Northlands Shopping Mall as the popular place to hang-out, but there was little else to do in the area, and certainly no youth-friendly options. This was a popular workshop and young people spent time designing their ideal youth facility.

At the end of the day, the network of youth workers had piles of butcher paper notes and plans. Collaborating on finding and equipping a youth facility was taken on as a priority by the group. A number of spaces to rent were checked out and a submission made to the City Council for funding to help cover the rent for a building. A well-documented case (including a business plan) was presented to the

Council by the network members along with young people. The Council agreed to underwrite the rental costs by $45,000 per year.

However, opportunities do not always come as we expect them to, and time after time possible venues fell through. Three years went by and still a youth facility was only a dream. By this time the local Baptist Church was making strong overtures for a Community Centre in the area and had become involved with the youth network. The church head-hunted and employed a dynamic youth worker to further their, and youth, interests in the area. Ross and I met numerous times over coffee in one of his favourite cafés in Northlands Mall. We met there so often that when we arranged a meeting via phone, Ross would say "I'll meet you at my office." I knew that meant his favourite café.

One day I got a phone call from a colleague of mine who worked as a Funding Adviser in the central Christchurch City Council offices. "Did you know that the Papanui Youth Facility account has $135,000 sitting in it, Bruce?" he asked. I almost fell off my chair. We had all forgotten the Council's commitment to underwriting the rental costs by $45,000 per year. After three years, that $45,000 had become $135,000. My first thought after putting the phone down was to ring Ross and suggest we meet in his "office."

"Do you think the Council would be amenable to that money being used as capital that could be used for purchasing somewhere instead of renting?" Ross asked. We decided to find out. Another deputation to the Council, again with a favourable outcome. Yes, they said, we could use the $135,000 as capital.

Over the next few months, favours were called in, connections and alliances made, business owners gave their time, and a friendly architect was engaged. Fundraising and donations towards the project began in earnest. Through it all Ross and I continued to meet in his "office" to drink coffee and to discuss progress. In all, over $1 million in funds or the equivalent in materials were donated.

Ross made contact with another church in the area and, after talking with the trustees and the local congregation, the St Paul's

Anglican Church allowed land at the back of their church building to be used for a purpose-built youth facility.

Eventually, almost nine years to the day after the Great North West Youth Summit, Te Koru Pou Iho (Papanui Youth Facility) was opened. The purpose-built facility contains a climbing wall, a recording studio, art room, computer suite, a fully-equipped kitchen and office space.

The facility is a remarkable example of collaboration (two churches - Baptist and Anglican, youth groups, Christchurch City Council, the local Community Board, local business leaders, Northlands Mall and numerous individuals.) It is also an example of the basic ideas outlined in this book: the Butterfly Effect, emergence, complexity, and just what can happen if we look for the opportunities that arise from simple, encouraging, conversations over cups of coffee.

V
COFFEE

Coffee: that ubiquitous bean from exotic lands and warm climes. The bittersweet taste of oriental flavours and Caribbean aromas. The word itself conjures up images, tastes, and smells. First thing in the morning bleary-eyed, or on a balcony in a balmy evening overlooking the ocean, coffee may well claim to be the elixir of life.

Coffee may also be the elixir of networks and relationship building. Social entrepreneurs, community development workers and social justice advocates all do their best work when working alongside and with others. Whatever the issue; carbon emissions, infant health or youth justice, we need to work together to find the creative solutions within increasingly complex environments.

Coffee also provides us with an easily memorised and useful acronym with which to explore these networks and relationships and the creative solutions that might emerge from them.

C.O.F.F.E.E. stands for:
> **C**reative
> **O**pportunities
> **F**low
> **F**rom
> **E**ncouraging
> **E**ncounters[©]

All six of these words can be explored as six separate ideas, but the power of the acronym is in the working of the six words in harmony. I will explore each one separately before discussing the acronym and concept as a whole.

Half a century ago those working for social change would most likely have met in the local tavern or pub over a pint of ale to discuss the ills of the world and how best to meet the needs of disadvantaged communities.

The analysis has changed in recent years with activators now more inclined to work from a strength or asset-based model. The venue for discussion has also changed. This century the public meeting place of choice has shifted from the local pub to the café down the road, with the choice of beverage now being a flat white, latte, cappuccino or long black.

So, pour yourself a coffee and discover how creative opportunities flow from encouraging encounters.

VI
CREATIVE

Albert Einstein is credited with one of the most often quoted observations about the way in which we humans attempt to solve problems. It is worth quoting again: *"We can't solve problems using the same thinking we used when we created them."*[11]

Indeed not, we need to become far more creative, more imaginative than we have been. If we want to get from A to B on a map then we do so by using logic and our analytical map reading skills. But if we want to draw the map then we need our creative abilities. We need to be open to new and unexpected insights, thoughts, ideas, and intuitions.

When we think of the word *creative* we often think of artists, musicians, dancers, performers, poets or writers. Certainly, these people must draw on their creative talents, but creativity is not the sole preserve of artists. All of us can be creative and here we are concerned with how we can use our collective creativity in order to prevent the coming multi-faceted emergency.

We may think that we are not creative. "Oh, I'm a left-brain person" we may say and so dismiss any possibility of creativity. However, the notion that creativity is only a right-brain activity is pure fiction. It is a myth. The problem is that if we come to believe the myth then it just may become a self-fulfilling belief, and so, prove

---

[11] It seems that Einstein never actually said this, although he was the Chairman of the Emergency Committee of Atomic Scientists who sent a telegram to hundreds of prominent Americans in May 1946, in which the following phrase was used: *"...a new type of thinking is essential if mankind is to survive and move toward higher levels."* This telegram came in the wake of the dropping of the atomic bombs on Hiroshima and Nagasaki and at a time of heightened nuclear tensions. Somehow that extract from the telegram came to be attributed to Einstein himself and re-formatted to the quotation about not being able to solve problems with the same thinking that created them. Certainly, when Einstein was interviewed a few months later he reiterated the quote from the telegram and said to the interviewer (Michael Amrine) *"We must abandon competition and secure cooperation."*

the myth to ourselves. Our brains are actually a lot more complex than the simple dualism of right brain – left brain that much of popular psychology has led us to believe. Indeed, activities like creativity (and rationality for that matter) are more whole-brain activities. (See box).

So, the first creative step that we may need to take on the path towards improved creativity is to discard the myth of creativity being a right-brained activity and only applicable to artists and other "creative" types. Similarly, those who enjoy a creative life should take heart in recognising that logic, analytical ability and other so-called left-brain functions are as accessible to them as they are to mathematicians or business analysts.

All of us have an imagination, all of us dream, all of us can tap into an intuitive space. Modern society, however, tells us that our imaginations and dreams are of little concern in a world in which economic systems predominate. The lot of many of us is to be consumers and/or producers in a dangerous system of continuing growth. If we fall for this purely

---

The Left Brain-Right Brain Myth

In the 1960s scientists cut the structure (corpus callosum) that connects the left and right brains of epilepsy sufferers in an attempt to cure them. They then looked at what sides of the brain were involved in language, maths, drawing etc., and found that one side was more likely to be involved in some functions than the other. Popular psychology took this to mean that we are all either left brain dominant or right brain dominant. But this failed to recognise that the experiments were with <u>unconnected</u> brain hemispheres, and neuroscientists have never held to the left-right brain myth. In 2013 researchers at the University of Utah studied the <u>connected</u> brains of more than 1,000 people and found that *"It is not the case that the left hemisphere is associated with logic or reasoning more than the right, (and that) creativity is no more processed in the right hemisphere than the left."*

Source: Nielsen JA, Zielinski BA, Ferguson MA, Lainhart JE, Anderson JS (2013) *An Evaluation of the Left-Brain vs. Right-Brain Hypothesis with Resting State Functional Connectivity Magnetic Resonance Imaging.* PLoS ONE 8(8): e71275.

economic definition then we become consumers, clients, patients, or audiences. We are all of these and more. We should defend our right to be known as citizens – full of potential, skills, and creative abilities.

Our job as social activators is to engage with people so as to break down culturally and economically imposed norms and awaken individual and collective imaginations. We are facilitators of processes that tap into the rich imaginations of a diversity of cultures, imaginations, skills and wisdom.

When those diverse imaginations and dreams are brought together to feed off one another then truly creative solutions can emerge. When we think of some of the emergencies mentioned earlier in this book, we can dream of a future in which those emergencies have dispersed.

Think of it this way: when we want to get data or information about the past then that is a fairly straight-forward activity. We use our research skills, our memories, or we consult expert witnesses. But to get data and information about the future we have to use our imaginations, we have to dream, we have to delve into our creativity.

How do we do that? What follows are some techniques or examples of what has worked to enable creative responses. However, please do not become limited to these approaches – after all, the purpose of creativity is to explore new ideas, to seek different ways of doing things.

Brainstorming

The technique of brainstorming has been with us for decades and possibly needs little explanation here other than to outline the process briefly:

1. The issue or question that the group is addressing is clarified, e.g. "how do we get the local council to provide safe and effective cycle lanes?"
2. The facilitator asks people to throw out ideas, no matter how crazy the idea may seem, *without comment or questions* from other members of the group. The facilitator writes each of these ideas onto a whiteboard or large sheet of paper.

3. The group continues brainstorming until such time as no more ideas are forthcoming. The facilitator can encourage more ideas by asking questions such as "anything else?" or "any other ideas, no matter how crazy?"
4. Note that no idea is excluded from being written down at this stage. You never know when an idea that may seem impractical or impossible to implement may spark an idea in someone else.
5. Once all ideas are out, the facilitator then asks if there are any questions of clarification. At this stage the ideas are not debated or considered, only clarified.
6. The group is then asked to combine ideas that seem to fit together. This makes the various ideas more manageable when it comes to working on how the ideas might be put into practice.
7. Only at this stage are the ideas subjected to analysis and debated as to their efficacy and/or worthiness. Depending upon the size of the group, it may be possible for the group to break into smaller groups and work on one or two of the combined ideas together and then present their findings back to the entire group.
8. During the analysis phase it is important to look at the idea from all perspectives, including those of "how can this work?" as much as "what makes this not work?"

A word or two of caution does need to be mentioned here. Much research into the use of brainstorming suggests that, contrary to expected results, brainstorming can lead to less inventive ideas than if people had been left to themselves to come up with creative ideas.[12] The reasons for this appear to be related to the trap of collective folly, which is addressed later in the book. The technique does still have value however, although some tweaking may be in order. Allowing

---

[12] I suspect that most of the studies of brainstorming referred to have studied groups that are homogeneous in nature. Within more diverse groups this objection may not be so valid.

time for people to work on their own before the group comes together may be useful. Asking group members to write down their ideas on post-it notes, for example, may be helpful. Even just allowing group members to have some individual time may be sufficient.

Lateral Thinking

Edward de Bono is perhaps the best known of thinkers on creative thinking and has been called "the father of lateral thinking." De Bono developed a number of techniques designed to stimulate lateral thinking. De Bono contrasted vertical thinking (the traditional, logical thinking process) with lateral thinking – a process that disrupts the vertical thinking sequence and arrives at a solution from another angle.

Some of de Bono's techniques are simple, such as the idea of picking two words at random out of a dictionary and then brainstorming how those two words are connected to each other and to the issue at hand.

Perhaps one of de Bono's most famous contributions to lateral thinking and the creative process is that of Six Thinking Hats.[13] Briefly, de Bono describes six differently coloured hats to symbolise the style of thinking that is embodied when the thinker has that hat on their head. The important element in de Bono's contribution is that all of us can place any of these hats on our head and utilise that style of thinking – we are not bound to just one or two styles.

- *White Hat*: This hat represents data and information. This hat asks "what do we know?" and "what do we need to find out?" Think of a white sheet of paper with facts and figures on it.
- *Blue Hat:* This is the hat that represents the big picture, the overview. Think of the blue sky and how overarching it is, the wider view.

---

[13] For a fuller, more complete, explanation of the Six Thinking Hats, see de Bono's books *Six Thinking Hats,* or *Serious Creativity.* Or visit his website (debonothinkingsystems.com) for training options.

- *Yellow Hat:* This is the hat of optimism. Whilst wearing this hat one looks for the positives and asks "how can this work?" Think of the yellow sun full of optimism.
- *Black Hat:* This hat is the opposite of the yellow one. The wearer of this hat asks "what are the risks and problems here?" Think of the Grim Reaper clothed in black.
- *Red Hat:* This is the hat of passion and feelings. The wearer of the red hat asks "what is my intuitive response?" "What do I feel about this idea?" Think of the red flames of passion.
- *Green Hat:* Wearing this hat suggests growth and creativity. It is the hat of possibilities and opportunities (see next chapter). The wearer asks "what are the alternatives?" Wearing this hat often has the advantage of seeing through the problems and risks identified when wearing the black hat. Think of green grass growing.

Lateral thinking (or thinking outside the box as it has sometimes been called – see also page 49) can sometimes be guided by the specific needs or conditions of the problem at hand. In 2010 in Colombia, Colonel Jose Espejo had just such a problem.

Colonel Espejo was due for retirement but he was haunted by the knowledge that sixteen Colombian soldiers remained in harsh captivity by Revolutionary Armed Forces of Colombia (FARC) guerrillas deep in the jungle. Espejo wanted to be able to get a message of hope to these men, most of them having been held in captivity for more than ten years. But the message had to get to the soldiers without their captors realising it. The solution required a creative approach. Espejo telephoned Juan Carlos Ortiz, an advertising genius who had gained fame by winning a Gold Lion (the advertising industry's version of an Oscar) at Cannes – the first Colombian to do so.

High above the streets of Bogota, Espejo, Ortiz and other creative Colombian advertising people met to brainstorm ideas. Espejo explained the situation and the problem. The Colombian army was conducting missions in the area and they wanted to alert the captives to be ready to escape at a moment's notice. But that message had to get to the captives without their captors being aware of it. Various ideas were bounced around. Alfonso Diaz blurted out "what about código Morse?" – Morse code. Espejo liked it. The soldiers were trained in Morse code, but their captors were unlikely to understand it. But how could they get the Morse to them? Maybe added onto the end of an advert on radio – the captives had access to radios; being one of the few luxuries permitted them. That idea was scrapped as it would be too obvious.

Then someone suggested embedding it into a song. As a young man Ortiz had been a musician so the idea of creating a song appealed to him. Lateral thinking had put together two ideas – Morse code and a song. The concept had potential. Radio Bemba, a small recording studio was approached and sworn to secrecy. Embedding the tell-tale dots and dashes of Morse code in a song proved to be not so easy. Eventually, the team discovered the perfect rhythm and number of dots and dashes to match it. The song, *Better Days*, was recorded with session musicians and the vocals of Natalia Gutierrez Y Angelo. Embedded within a bridge between verses were the Morse code dots and dashes spelling out the message, *"19 people rescued. You're next. Don't lose hope."*[14]

By December 2010 the song was being played on more than 130 small, rural, radio stations and listened to by over 3 million people, and had become very popular. Within two years all the hostages had been freed or released. Upon being freed, one of the hostages spoke of hearing the hidden message in the song and that the message had been passed from hostage to hostage.

In 2011 the Colombian army declassified the operation and allowed the song to be entered into the Cannes Lions. Juan Carlos Ortiz now has two Gold Lions adorning his offices.

What can we learn from this inspiring story? It is creative, of that there can be no doubt. Admittedly, those at the centre of the creativity were advertising people, and that is what they are paid to be.

---

[14] Listen to the song at www.youtube.com/watch?v=7CqOYM7cCX8

But this problem was more than advertising a product. This had very strict requirements. It was a specific message. It had to convey that message to those that needed to hear it, yet keep it hidden from those that weren't to hear it. It required lateral thinking. Crucially, it required receptive minds open to thinking outside the box. Imagine the scene. An army colonel in a large room is concerned to get a crucial message to captive soldiers, and someone says *"how about a song?"* If Colonel Espejo had not had an open, receptive mind, this operation would have failed before it got to the first note

Question, question, question

To quote Einstein again: *"The important thing is to not stop questioning. Curiosity has its own reason for existing."*

Warren Berger has written extensively on the art of questioning. His book *A More Beautiful Question* explores in depth the art and science of asking profound questions – questions that open up space for fresh ideas and creative thinking. Often, says Berger, we do not need to tackle everything at once, we could start with the simple question: *"what if I (we) made one small change?"* Too often we get bogged down in trying to solve everything at once, whereas asking "what is the one small thing we can do now?" may be more appropriate and may lead to further questions and answers.

As children we constantly asked questions: "Why is the sky blue?" "Why does grandad use a walking stick?" "Why do I have to go in the car?" Indeed, by the age of four we are asking around 300 questions each and every day. Between two and five years of age most children will have asked 40,000 questions.

But then, during our elementary, or primary, school years we stop asking questions. Our education system teaches us that answers are more important than questions, so we are discouraged from asking questions. Disturbingly, there is some evidence to suggest that teachers, in general, have a bias towards less creative students. This "don't ask" creed gets carried on into adult life. Our early working life experience is often peppered with phrases such as "this is the way it is done here. What gives you the right to question it?"

Yet, asking questions has been fundamental to our individual and collective development. If we hadn't been able to ask questions it is difficult to imagine how humans would have ever discovered how to light fires, invent the wheel or paint the ceiling of the Sistine Chapel.

Asking questions stimulates our curiosity. For this reason alone, questioning is a practice that we should encourage in ourselves. Recent research indicates that being curious has at least four benefits for each of us.

1. When we are curious we are motivated to learn and we become better learners.
2. Our curiosity stimulates our personal growth and also deepens the connections we make with people when we first meet them.
3. Our sense of personal meaning and purpose in life is heightened when we are curious. There is always something new to explore, discover, or learn.
4. Curiosity stimulates and strengthens the brain. As it is for muscles, the more we use the brain the healthier it remains. What exercise could be better for the brain than that of being curious, continually asking questions?

But it is not only for our own personal benefit that questioning is valuable. In terms of our social development, if it hadn't been for social innovators like William Wilberforce asking questions in parliament we would not have ended slavery. If Copernicus, Galileo and others hadn't questioned the accepted doctrines of the time we would still be looking up to the heavens thinking that everything revolved around us. If we still believed that we could not land on the moon, we would not have the worldwide communications and global positioning systems we have today.

When we question things and find out an answer, we find that we then have more questions. In fact, it is a truism that when we question things we discover that we know less and less. As Aristotle said, more than 2,300 years ago: *"The more you know, the more you know you don't know."* Here's a question: why is that? Why, when we get answers to our questions, is it that we have lots more questions? Have a look at the diagram below.

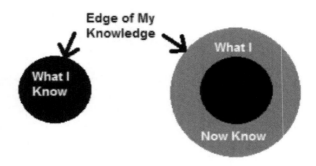

On the left side of the diagram, if everything I know is represented by the black circle, then what I don't know is all outside that circle. The edge of my knowledge is the circumference of the circle. It is at the circumference that I question things. I ask: "What is beyond the circumference?"

Now, what happens when I get answers to my questions? See the right side of the diagram. The answers to my questions have expanded the circle of "what I know."

But, in the expansion of my circle of knowledge, what happens to the circumference – the edge of my knowledge? As we can see, it has grown. The circumference is now longer than it was. I have an expanded circle of knowledge, but my knowledge of what I don't know is now much greater.

This knowledge paradox is one of the reasons that we need to seek diversity in working with the emergencies that face us. No one of us can ever know the entire landscape. None of us has all the answers. Indeed, crucially, none of us has all the questions.

Inner Listening

To be creative we need to develop our listening skills in two ways. First, to be able to fully utilise our collective creativity we must learn to listen to one another. Listening in this way is not simply sitting without saying anything, waiting until there is a space for us to fill with our own thoughts and ideas. I will return to this theme in the chapter on **Encouraging** as the discussion on listening to one another fits more comfortably there. (See pp 94-98) The second listening skill that we need to develop is our inner listening;

For centuries indigenous cultures have retained a connection with deep inner listening that we in the western-styled cultures have largely lost, ignored, or had stolen from us. If we stop to listen and learn from indigenous cultures we may find that something is stirred or resonates within our own psyche. The Aboriginal culture of Australia is one of those where inner listening has remained an important ingredient of the culture.

Miriam-Rose Ungunmerr is a Ngangikurungkurr woman from northern Australia. Miriam Rose describes the word *dadirri*[15] from her language as, *"inner, deep listening and quiet, still awareness. Dadirri recognises the deep spring that is inside us. We call on it and it calls to us. This is the gift that Australia is thirsting for. It is something like what you call "contemplation". When I experience dadirri, I am made whole again. I can sit on the riverbank or walk through the trees; even if someone close to me has passed away, I can find my peace in this silent awareness. There is no need of words. A big part of dadirri is listening. Through the years, we have listened to our stories. They are told and sung, over and over, as the seasons go by. Today we still gather around the campfires and together we hear the sacred stories."*

Indigenous people all over the world will relate to this beautiful word picture of Miriam-Rose. We in the west may be

---

[15] The word, concept and spiritual practice that is *dadirri* is from the Ngan'gikurunggurr and Ngen'giwumirri languages of the Aboriginal peoples of the Daly River region (Northern Territory, Australia).

starting to re-discover this contemplation of our inner silence through our growing appreciation of the role of intuition in our lives.

It is worth noting that intuition is not a magical process whereby an idea or answer just pops into our head out of nowhere. Intuition is literally learning from within: in-tuition. Intuition is *"nothing more and nothing less than recognition"* according to the psychologist Herbert A Simon.

Intuition is often accompanied by an "ah-hah" type response, signalling that the intuitive idea is characterised by a feeling of familiarity. In fact, during the 1970s, a group of Canadian churches combined to form GATT-Fly, a project to carry out research, education and action in solidarity with people's organisations in Canada and throughout the world to work for global economic justice. They developed an empowering educational technique based on exactly this response – calling it the "Ah-Hah Seminar."[16] The technique draws heavily on the work of Brazilian educator Paulo Freire and "helps groups do their own analysis by providing a

---

Ah-Ha Seminar

Briefly, the Ah-Ha Seminar uses a dialogical approach to learning whereby the participants in the seminar collectively draw a picture, using symbols, to depict their world, how that world operates and who are the various stakeholders and decision-makers. The seminar approach turns on its head the traditional education approach, whereby an educator teaches learners what the educator wishes them to know. Paulo Freire terms this the "banking" model of education which assumes that learners are empty vessels that need to be filled with information, skills and ideas. The Ah-Ha Seminar encourages participants to work with their own experience and discover the learning that they already have.

In an Ah-Ha Seminar the role of the facilitator is to use questions that enable participants to describe their lives, draw out themes that emerge, discover a larger picture and make global connections. As this picture develops participants often come to a sudden ah-ha moment and exclaim something like: "ah – so that's it," "it all suddenly fits into place" or "it's dawned on me that..." The process enables what we already know intuitively to become explicit.

---

[16] GATT-Fly, 1983, 1986.

structure and some tools to accomplish this task." The technique is an overtly political one as the process is designed to help participants analyse a situation or issue in order to change it. That makes it a technique worth mentioning in this book (see box).

How do we develop our intuition? Most writers on the topic seem to agree that there are four barriers that we need to overcome:

1. Declutter your mind. Tapping into your inner wisdom is difficult if there is a lot of clutter in the way. You will find your own way to declutter; some ways are to go for a walk, get into nature, listen to music or meditate. Perhaps a shower. Have you noticed how often you'll get a good idea in the shower? It's surprisingly common.[17] Whatever you do, you need to give your mind freedom.
2. Ignore what you know. Intuition deals more with feelings, insights and emotions than it does with facts and figures. This does not mean that you reject the facts and figures, just put them aside and ask yourself how you feel about the question, issue or problem? How is your body responding?
3. Get out of your head. Go with your gut. Often we get a "gut feeling" before our brain takes over and becomes the "knower." Get in tune with your gut. Do your stomach muscles contract and tighten or do they relax? Does your heart and chest feel as if it is expanding?
4. Let go the need to control. Our rational mind tells us that we should be in control at all times. However, when we wish to tap into our intuition we need to surrender this desire and trust that our intuition will provide us with insights without our need to dictate what those insights might be.

---

[17] Research by the German bathroom and kitchen fixtures company Hansgrohe SE, in 2014, found that 72% of 4,000 people surveyed from 8 countries reported new insights whilst standing in a shower. Scott Barry Kaufman Ph.D. (the researcher) comments that *"It's both surprising and fascinating to learn that people are more creative in the shower than they are at work, with Hansgrohe's findings reinforcing existing research on the importance of relaxation for creative thinking."*

Once we have decluttered, ignored what we know, and told our heads to go west, there are some practices that can stimulate and encourage intuitive thinking:

1. Look for patterns and connections between things. In many ways the world is a series of patterns, many of which we don't notice because we are not looking for them. As soon as we deliberately look we just may find that we notice things in quite a different way. Dr Wayne Dyer notes that when you *"change the way you look at things, then the things you look at change."*

2. When you get flights of fancy or find yourself daydreaming, go with it. You never know where it may take you.

3. Does what you're looking at, or thinking about, remind you of something else? How are they similar? How are they dissimilar? What would happen if you put them together?

4. Do you remember the word association games that children used to play (and psychologists prompted us with)? Pick a word – what associations arise? What associations arise from there? Keep going; use a stream of consciousness approach.

5. Metaphors, analogies and allegories are great ways to explore ideas. Using our intuition allows a metaphor to be expanded and take on new meanings, where the rational mind might want to contain the image within "realistic" bounds.

6. Speculate; ask "what if" type questions.

7. Imagine, imagine, imagine. Write a story, but don't make it about something or somebody (including yourself) that you already know. Create a character (with a name, an age, a gender ...), put them into some unusual situation, and then just see what happens. Do they interact with other characters? What do they say? How do they act? Instead of writing a story, paint or draw a picture. Just imagine; use colour, use shape, use texture.

8. Read poetry, visit an art gallery. Let the words or the images flow into your consciousness. Try to not "think" about the poem or painting. How does your gut react? How about your heart? How does the poem or painting make you feel?

In many ways intuition can be tapped into via any of the "four windows of knowing" as psychologist Eligio Gallegos names them: feeling, imagining, sensing, thinking. In each of these modalities our intuition can be of an aid to our creativity. For example, we may get a feeling that something might work, or that we get an urge to talk to a particular person. We may be sitting on a hilltop watching the clouds and our imagination begins to make shapes of those clouds and then our intuition tells us that we should follow that imagination. Perhaps we hear the call of a bird and our intuition kicks in and tells us that it is a warning call and we need to pay attention to something. Or we can be deeply into a thought and suddenly our intuition tells us to take the second of two options that we were thinking about. Thus, intuition can arise by looking through any, or all, of these four windows – it is not simply via our feelings only, as is sometimes commonly thought.

Before moving on, I want to briefly discuss the difference between intuition and instinct. Instinct is a biological impulse – a reaction within us that stereotypically makes us fight, flee or freeze. Often it is unconscious and more often than not, uncontrollable: we respond without thinking about our response, and before we know it we are running for our lives.

Intuition, on the other hand, is conscious. Intuition provides us with information that we then consider. Intuition may tell us that one course of action is more appealing to us than another, but we still have the ability to choose to follow that advice or not.

Intuition can aid our creativity. Instinct, however, does not.

Make Mistakes, Learn to Fail

One of our biggest barriers to creativity is the fear of failure.[18] This doesn't mean that we should ignore the risks; it just means that we must break through emotional and/or psychological barriers that often leave us unable to do anything. Symptoms of this fear can

---

[18] Here's a new word for those of you who like words. Atichyphobia is the abnormal, unwarranted and persistent fear of failure.

include; a reluctance to try anything new, anxiety, a low sense of worth, or perfectionism (whereby we are willing to do only those things that we know we can succeed at).

However, history abounds with stories of inventors, scientists, artists and others who failed numerous times before succeeding. Here are just three examples of such stories.

Thomas Edison, the inventor of the light bulb, reputedly tried 1,000 different filaments for his light bulb, none of which worked. The story goes that a journalist queried him on this and asked why he didn't give up after 1,000 failures. Edison famously replied, *"I haven't failed 1,000 times, I've just proven 1,000 ways in which it doesn't work."*

Michael Jordan is credited with being the greatest basketballer to have ever lived. Here is what he had to say about failure and success: *"I have missed more than 9,000 shots in my career. I have lost almost 300 games. On 26 occasions I have been entrusted to take the game-winning shot, and I missed. I have failed over and over and over again in my life. And that is why I succeed."*

The story of Robert the Bruce and the spider is well known, even if it may be clouded in fiction. The story goes that during his reign as King of Scotland Bruce was defeated by the English and fled to a cave. There he sat and watched a spider trying to spin a web. The spider kept failing but didn't give up. Eventually, as Bruce watched, the spider managed to stick a strand of silk to the cave wall and so build its web. Bruce took this as a sign (if at first you don't succeed, try and try again) and went on to defeat the English at the Battle of Bannockburn in 1314.

In his book The Power of Failure[19] Charles Manz defines failure as, *"a short-term unexpected result that reflects a challenge in progress and that provides: a stepping stone to success, an opportunity for learning and development, (and) an opportunity for creative change and innovation."*

---

[19] Charles C Manz. 2009.

Note how Manz connects failure with creativity and innovation. For readers interested in exploring the power of failure, Manz's book lists 27 mechanisms for overcoming the fear of failure and for recognising that within failure is the seed of success. These 27 mechanisms are categorised into 8 themes. Manz says that the first step is to redefine what we mean by failure. Instead of thinking that failure means that we are somehow inept, lacking or deficient, we must come up with a redefinition which understands failure as stepping stones towards success, and that within the failure is an opportunity to learn and create something new in our lives.

Redefining failure in this way means that we also must redefine success so that success is not seen as a final state. Instead, success is redefined as being a continuous journey of discovery, learning, and invention. Within that journey there will be setbacks as well as triumphs. Success in this definition lies in the onward journey, not the final destination. The key to enjoying this journey is being persistent, just as Thomas Edison, Michael Jordan, and Robert the Bruce were.

When we undertake a journey such as this we are bound to receive negative comments and feedback (as Edison did from the journalist.) This can be discouraging and/or upsetting, but Manz recommends that we use this feedback to find a way to turn the negative into a positive. He suggests further that when we receive negative comment it may actually indicate that we are onto something new and original. Perhaps we have begun a journey that others have so far been unwilling to undertake, and the negativity could be a display of the tall poppy syndrome.[20]

Within each apparent failure there are lessons to be learnt and new opportunities present themselves. Understanding this it becomes possible to view each failure as a stepping stone towards success. However, this should not mean that we do not accept responsibility for "true failures." If something truly does not work, or it has

---

[20] *Tall poppy syndrome* is a phrase used extensively in the UK, Australia, and New Zealand to describe a propensity to attack, criticise, or run-down someone within the culture who has achieved well, or somehow stood out (like a tall poppy).

unintentionally harmed someone then it is important to acknowledge this, take responsibility, and admit the mistake.

Success, according to Manz, should not be seen as an individual accomplishment that is pursued for personal fame, fortune or power. Manz is at pains to note that we need to look outside ourselves when thinking about success. In an apparent paradox, Manz notes that when we help others succeed, even at our own expense, we become less vulnerable to feelings of failure.

Creativity breeds creativity

"Creativity can be contagious, it can create a climate for mobilising more creative potential." Voula Mega[21]

Just as someone smiling at another person can elicit a smile in the other, so creativity has a habit of eliciting creativity in other people. Look at the example of the "Umbrella Revolution" in Hong Kong in late 2014. At first, just a few "artists" created public and political art, but it soon spread to thousands of young people on the streets of Hong Kong discovering their creativity and expressing it.

Furthermore, you don't need to be creative in order to be creative. That sounds ridiculous and illogical, doesn't it? However, sometimes it is not the person who comes up with a new idea who is the creative one. It may be the person listening who realises that the new idea has great potential, and who then goes on to explore the idea further and find ways to put it into practice. Thus, the creative person may be the one who sees the opportunities that emerge from our encounters rather than the one who expressed the idea initially. So, don't feel as if you have to be searching for creative ideas all the time, waiting for the light bulb to go off inside your head. It may be that someone has expressed an idea and your creative ability is to notice the creativity inherent in that idea.

---

[21] Quoted in Westoby & Dowling, p 52. Voula Mega is the author of a number of books on sustainable cities.

Think Inside the Box

How many of you have heard the phrase "think outside the box" as a way to tap into your creative potential? That may be a useful metaphor for lateral thinking, but so too could be the exhortation to think inside the box.

If you think of the box as the container within which all your attributes, skills, ideas, and information are found, then it may be that your next creative idea is already inside the box. Einstein and others often spoke of creativity being a process whereby the new idea is simply a combination of pre-existing components, put together in a new way. Einstein called this "combinatorial play." The more you have inside the box, the more relationships between them are possible.

So, don't think "I have to think differently in order to be creative." It may be that you already have enough stuff inside the box for you to play with and come up with new, imaginative and inspirational combinations.

Thinking outside the box comes from the 9-dot puzzle. The goal of the puzzle is to link all 9 dots using four straight lines or fewer, without lifteing the pen and without tracing the same line more than once.

A solution will be offered at the end of the book (p 161).

Improvisation

Anyone who has attended a Playback Theatre performance, or watched the television show *Whose Line Is It Anyway?* will have roared with laughter at the antics of the actors as they act out, without pre-prepared scripts, scenes, situations and scenarios from the random suggestions of the audience. Those of us in the audience marvel at the ingenuity, spontaneity, and creativity the actors bring to the performance. How do they do it, we may ask?

Can we adopt the ideas of improvisation (Improv as it has come to be known in its theatrical setting) for our own explorations of creativity? The answer, according to at least one Improv teacher and writer is a resounding "yes." Improv, says Patricia Ryan Madson, is based on 13 very simple maxims.

1. Say Yes. Saying yes means being open to what is happening, going with the flow, being open to the opportunities that arise. Saying yes builds on the ideas already in existence. Saying no, on the other hand, can be a desire to control the flow, which then leads to everyone being stifled.
2. Don't Prepare. Too much planning can block being in the present; it can distract from listening to others.
3. Just Show Up. Just be there, make the effort. Woody Allen is reputed to have remarked that *"eighty percent of success is showing up."*
4. Start Anywhere. We can lose focus, energy, or time by trying to figure out where to start. Indeed, worrying about where to start can lead to never starting at all.
5. Be Average. There is no need to strive for perfection (it's not possible anyway), just be natural. Bring who you are to the situation, not who you think you ought to be.
6. Pay Attention. Although being aware of your own thoughts, ideas and feelings are helpful, being overly focussed on them can mean missing the opportunities that are offered by other people or the situation.
7. Face The Facts. Worrying about the future is pointless, so too is agonising over the past. Mark Twain, with characteristic wit, noted that *"Some of the worst things in my life never happened."* Things may not be ideal but they are what they are.
8. Stay The Course. Keep with it. Keep in mind the purpose, not what you are doing or even the goal. The purpose of meeting with someone, or acting with others, is far more important than the goal you have set yourself. How many times have we heard the phrase *"lifes higher purpose"* and then neglected it to think about our immediate goals instead?

9. Wake Up To The Gifts. Opportunities are everywhere, be open to them. (See next Chapter)
10. Make Mistakes, Please. An earlier subsection of this chapter looked at the creative opportunities that exist in our mistakes. But be wary: this is not an excuse for slip shoddiness.
11. Act Now. This maxim focuses on acting, not doing. Sometimes the best action may be doing nothing, or simply observing.
12. Take Care Of Each Other. This maxim is very much the focus of the chapter on Encouraging (see p 86f). Share and share alike.
13. Enjoy The Ride. Not everything is fun, but we can still enjoy the moment, the situation, the company, for what it is. When we come from a place within us that is joyful, then almost any situation is tolerable. We cannot have excitement in our lives all the time, but we can enliven our lives.

There it is – thirteen simple maxims for improvisation. Yet, from these simple ideas some wonderful, creative, and elaborate ideas can spring.

Collective Creativity

This book focuses on collective approaches to dealing creatively with the complex world. However, much of what is written about creativity emphasises the creativity of individuals. Even Edward de Bono (the father of lateral thinking) veers towards being dismissive of collective approaches to creativity. In his book, *Serious Creativity,* he claims that [22] *"Individuals on their own can pursue many different directions. There is no need to talk and no need to listen. An individual on his or her own can pursue an idea that seems 'mad' at first and can stay with the idea until it makes sense. This is almost impossible to do in a group."*

---

[22] de Bono, Edward 1992.

He also states that *"In my experience individuals are much better at initiating ideas and opening up entirely new directions."*

In these statements de Bono assumes that the purpose of creativity is to solve or fix a problem, neglecting the benefits of working together – a benefit that may, in the long run, turn out to be of far more importance than solving the issue at hand. (I will have more to say on this in the final chapters of this book.) Hence de Bono misses the creative opportunity of people coming together to collaborate and share experience, skills, and ideas. In doing so, de Bono is furthering the myth that only certain individuals can be creative (although he would dispute this).

In the quote above it is noteworthy also that de Bono states that *"there is no need to talk and no need to listen."* This is unfortunate because talking and listening (conversing, dialoguing, communicating) may just be the very activities and skills that we need more of in the world if we are to find the creative opportunities to address the multi-emergencies facing us.

To de Bono's credit, he does go on to note that groups *"may have an advantage once the idea has been initiated. The members of the group may be able to flesh out the new idea and also to develop it in directions that might not have been considered by the originator of the idea."*

Taking note of de Bono's hesitation we can identify some barriers to collective creativity:[23]

- A desire to conform to group norms. If group members prize harmony over encouraging their fellows to offer differing opinions, then creativity can be hard to come by.
- Some groups may have no history or experience of working together and so a collaborative approach becomes difficult to achieve. It may be that members are used to a competitive culture and so will be suspicious of a more cooperative style.

---

[23] These barriers are adapted from McGraw Hill Education, http://www.mhhe.com/socscience/comm/group/students/creativity.htm accessed 4 April 2016

- If the working patterns amongst members are ones of making judgments, being critical or constant evaluation, then the openness and transparency required for creativity will be elusive.
- Some group members are more inclined towards the introversion end of the spectrum and so if those of an extroverted persuasion become more dominant in the group, then those who are more introspective or tentative about sharing their views will tend to switch off and not offer their ideas or insights. (See p 105-106)

Many of these barriers can be overcome by introducing diversity into the mix of minds attempting to work on an emergency. This book encourages the use of diversity, indeed, stresses the need for diversity when tackling some of the emergencies we face in our complex world. With diversity not only do we get differing experiences and skills, but also lesser adherence to cultural and group norms.

When de Bono wrote his book (1992), many of the inspirational, well-known examples of creative genius were those of individual people. Think of Einstein, da Vinci, Wollstonecraft, Monet, Edison, the Brontë sisters, Gandhi, Curie, or Newton. All of these primarily worked alone, although Isaac Newton did acknowledge that *"if I have seen further, it is by standing on the shoulders of giants."*[24] However, the author of a book on imagination, James Lehrer, notes that in science at least, the problems are becoming more complex and *"the low-hanging fruit is gone, and so we've got to learn to succeed together or fail alone."*[25]

In complex situations we cannot rely on individuals coming up with creative responses. We have to discover the mechanisms needed to collaborate and come up with collective creative responses.

---

[24] Isaac Newton in a letter to Robert Hooke, 15 February 1676.
[25] Interview with Jonah Lehrer.
http://greatergood.berkeley.edu/article/item/how_to_foster_group_creativity
Accessed 9 July 2016.

It appears that one of the keys to enhancing group creativity is simply generating a culture of creativity. When we live in a culture that values creativity, we will get greater creativity in both individual and group settings.

Hence, a further creative action that an activator can take is encouraging, fostering and promoting creativity. As noted earlier, creativity breeds creativity.

Creativity and Technological Innovation

Before moving from a discussion of creativity to the next facet of the **COFFEE** acronym I would like to further consider the quotation from Albert Einstein that began this chapter. Einstein, and the committee of scientists that he chaired referred to needing to change the thinking *style* that created the issues and problems that we are now faced with. Delving into Einstein's insight we discover that continuing to innovate using the same, world-weary, thinking that we have always used is not only insufficient, it is downright dangerous. Let me state it clearly: technological innovation is not the creativity that is being suggested in this book.

Innovation has come to be a bit of a catch-phrase, almost a beacon of hope, since the beginning of the twenty-first century. The concept arose within technological (especially software technology), business, and economic fields. More recently it has sneaked into community and social change environments. Innovation has been defined as,[26] *"production or adoption, assimilation, and exploitation of a value-added novelty in economic and social spheres; renewal and enlargement of products, services, and markets; development of new methods of production; and establishment of new management systems. It is both a process and an outcome."* One commentator has suggested that innovation requires three things: a need, relevant technology, and financial support. These are descriptions of the

---

[26] Edison, Ali, and Torkar, *Towards innovation measurement in the software industry, Journal of Systems and Software* 86(5), 2013. Sourced from Wikipedia, 14 October 2016

business-as-usual scenario that still continues to produce the emergencies that face us.

When innovation is examined from such definitions and requirements it becomes clear that technical innovation is not the new thinking that Einstein was talking about. In December 1917 he wrote to his friend, Heinrich Zangger, that *"All of our exalted technological progress, civilization for that matter, is comparable to an axe in the hand of a pathological criminal."* Einstein was talking about a creativity that radically shifts not just what we think and create, but how we think, and also what we think about. Einstein was talking about a thinking/creativity style that more closely speaks of consciousness and of who we are, rather than what we do.

When we stop to reconsider our thinking style then we can soon begin to shift towards thinking with our hearts and guts as much as with our heads. Heart-centred thinking is, *"independent, creative, moral and compassionate…it reflectively questions assumptions, discerns hidden values, and considers the larger social and ecological context. Heart-centred thinking is distinguished by an animated curiosity that leads to a constantly adjusting, in-depth knowledge of the environment, the human culture, and its individual members."*[27]

Heart-centred thinking, and the creativity that goes with it is closer to the new style of thinking that Einstein is exhorting us to encompass.

The emergencies that face us cannot be solved using innovation and technology. Indeed, often the use of technology and technically innovative styles of thinking lead us to further emergencies. I am reminded of the children's ditty about the old lady and the fly. *"I know an old lady who swallowed a fly/I don't know why she swallowed the fly/Perhaps she'll die."* The old lady goes on to swallow a spider to catch the fly. She keeps swallowing bigger and bigger creatures (a bird, a cat, a dog …) in order to solve the problem made by the previously swallowed creature. Most children know that the story does not end happily. *"I know an old lady who swallowed a*

---

[27] Bill Plotkin, 2013

horse/She's dead of course." We are doing the same with our reliance on technology and continued innovation. We cannot continue to solve problems with the same thinking with which we created them.

Unlike the old lady in the ditty, we have to stop our present ways of thinking and find new, far more creative, ways to think of and address the emergencies. In fact, it may be that the desire to "solve" problems is unhelpful and perhaps even part of the problem.

In the northern winter of 2000 four leading organisational learning thinkers sat in Massachusetts discussing theories of change and learning. Peter Senge, Otto Scharmer, Joseph Jaworski and Betty Sue Flowers eventually published a remarkable book based on their discussions.[28] Remarkable mainly due to the simple challenges they presented to mainstream organisational thinking. One of the basic tenets of organisational thinking they challenged was the notion of problem-solving. They noted that; *"The problem-solving mindset can be adequate for technical problems. But it can be woefully inadequate for complex human systems, where problems often arise from unquestioned assumptions and deeply habitual ways of acting. Until people start to see their own handprint on such problems, fundamental change rarely occurs."*

Western societies' tendency toward technological solutions has allowed these societies to prosper and grow in many areas. However, we have come to rely more and more on technological fixes, so much so that the technological solution becomes the default "go to" solution. Peter Senge tells the story of when he was presenting to a systems conference and he had a "blinding flash of the obvious." Senge realised that by doing so we "shift the burden" towards technological solutions at the expense of developing our collective human capacity and wisdom.[29] Shifting the burden in this way has a two-pronged weakness. As noted above, technological innovation may be helping to produce the very emergencies we wish to tackle. Lamentably it may also be distracting us from exploring our

---

[28] Senge, Peter et al
[29] Ibid

more creative depths, leading us further and further away from our collective wisdom. Worse still, shifting the burden to technological innovation may actually be blinding us to the real emergency – the alienation of our sense of self as an integral part of nature. (See pp 134f)

As we journey further into the **COFFEE** acronym you will find that questioning assumptions and habitual ways of doing things are presented as ways to think about how we encourage and encounter one another so that creative opportunities and wisdom can emerge.

VII
OPPORTUNITIES

The word opportunity derives from two old Latin words: *Ob* meaning towards and *portus* meaning a harbour. Literally then, opportunity represents movement towards a favourable place.

Opportunities surround us, but they only become real when we actively and positively seek or recognise them. We must become receptive to their presence and open to what they have to offer us. Opportunities arise, they are not forced or planned. If we are open and receptive we will see and hear opportunities wherever we look and listen. If we remain closed and unreceptive we will miss them or even deliberately ignore them. We often hear the saying "opportunity knocks only once." In order to ensure that opportunity doesn't give up and leave, we have to get up out of our comfortable chair and go to the door.

Community development has a history of seeking opportunity. The strand of community development known as Asset Based Community Development (ABCD) is strongly connected to the idea of seeking and acting on opportunities. Asset Based Community Development, as the name suggests, begins with the recognition that communities are asset rich (contrary to the needs-based approach of older community development models). Peter Kenyon, an Australian based advocate for and practitioner of ABCD, often puts up a slide similar to the picture at right when talking at conferences. He then asks the

audience how many of them think of this as the glass half-full and how many think of it as half-empty. He then suggests that the glass is both; half-full and half-empty. "But," he says, "you can't do much with the top half." It is the bottom half where ABCD goes seeking the skills, knowledge, and wisdom of the community. This is where the opportunities lie.

ABCD is rather like this description of the difference between an optimist and a pessimist: *"The pessimist sees the difficulty in every opportunity. An optimist, on the other hand, sees the opportunity in every difficulty."*[30]

Finding opportunity depends largely on your perspective. Opportunities are never overt or glaring you in the face. They are often hidden just out of sight. If we don't see the opportunities that emerge from our interaction with others, then we must go looking for them.

Within the context of this book, the opportunities that we are seeking are those that assist in overcoming one or more of the emergencies facing us or help us to see more clearly the links between the emergencies. Opportunities like these lead toward the emergence we desire.

When we begin a conversation, a community dialogue or even an international symposium with a mindset that sees others as holders of knowledge, skills, and wisdom and not as needy, uneducated or dim-witted, then we allow for new and exciting opportunities and possibilities to emerge from the discussion.

When we deliberately engage with others, and especially with those we would not normally engage – the stranger – then the dialogue can give rise to new and unexpected opportunities. Globalisation may be one of the causes of the emergencies imperilling us, but it also gives us access to a huge diversity of cultures with their attendant wisdom. At present much of the wisdom that is held within the world is untapped, unused and deliberately ignored in the global (and often local) search for solutions. Indigenous peoples have a

---

[30] Attributed to Winston Churchill

wealth of knowledge and wisdom that spans aeons and generations – yet it is missing from the global summits and conferences. At local levels too, indigenous knowledge is often ignored at worst or acknowledged with only a token consultative process. The Canadian anthropologist Robin Ridington reminds us that aboriginal people *"...are real. They are translators. They remember. We forget or ignore what they know at our peril."[31]*

Women are also largely missing from our public decision-making bodies. Men continue to occupy the highest levels of authority in government, business, finance and the think-tanks of the world. Again, the world loses many opportunities each and every day that women are excluded from public decision-making.

Furthermore, when we look at those who represent us in parliaments, senates, and congresses around the world we find a disturbing trend. We find that the sectors from which those "representatives" are drawn are becoming less and less... representative. Increasingly, our elected representatives come from the professional sectors of society including business, finance, education and law. The number of media and sports celebrities too is climbing higher and higher within our public decision-making bodies. Most distressing, however, is the advent of the career politician. An Australian study released in 2013 showed that during the 1940s just one percent of Members of Parliament (MPs) had previously worked in politics. By the early 21st Century that figure had mushroomed to a whopping 28%.

Thus, at the very time in our history when we need to draw on our diversity in order to discover the opportunities available to us, we are witnessing an increasing homogeneity in our public decision-makers.

This all points to the necessity of those seeking social change or working for community development, to proclaim the need for diversity.

---

[31] Quoted in Knudtson & Suzuki, p16.

Opportunity from Adversity

There is a story about a goat that fell down a well and began bleating in alarm. The farmer, hearing the goat's forlorn cries arrived at the well and looked in. The goat was at the very bottom, well beyond any ladder or other means of retrieving the poor animal. The farmer looked at the goat and decided that the goat was old anyway and was doomed to a miserable death at the bottom of the well. He decided to bury the goat in the well, and hurried off to his neighbours to ask them to come and help him bury the goat. His neighbours arrived with spades and shovels. The goat by this time was bleating and braying loudly and plaintively. The farmer and the neighbours began shovelling dirt into the well. After a while the goat's plaintive bleats turned to whinnies of delight. The farmer, confused by this, looked over the edge of the well as his neighbours continued to toss shovelfuls of dirt into the well. Each time one of those shovelfuls landed on the goat's back, the goat would shake itself and step up on the new layer of dirt. The farmer and neighbours continued shovelling. The goat kept shaking itself and stepping up to the new level. Eventually, the goat stepped out of the well and trotted off happily into the paddock.

The goat had found an opportunity in adversity.

In 2016 I was working in the area of restorative justice, a community-based sentencing process that brings together offenders, victims, support people, and members of the local community to talk about how people were affected by the offending, and then to come up with a plan that becomes the offender's sentence. One of the cases I worked on involved a young Aboriginal man from northern Australia. He was now living on the Mid North Coast of New South Wales, a quite different tribal grouping and language.[32] Monti (not his real name) was charged with resisting arrest and was referred to my case load.

---

[32] Prior to European colonisation there were over 250 distinct language groups in Australia. By the 21st century less than 150 of these are spoken, with 110 or more of them critically endangered.

Monti and his Gumbaynggirr[33] partner had two young children at the time of the offence. She and the children had been emotionally distressed by what had happened and the continuing presence of the justice system in their lives. She joined Monti, supporters, the arresting police officer, and a local Gumbaynggirr elder and CEO of a language and culture centre, in the restorative justice conference.

After almost two hours of honest, sometimes emotional, but always respectful conversation a sentencing plan for Monti was adopted by consensus by all concerned. One of the outcomes of the plan was that Monti would undertake a year-long course of language and cultural learning at the language and culture centre. The sentencing plan was presented to the presiding magistrate and accepted.

Two weeks later I sat down with Monti (over a coffee – of course) to discuss how he would begin and maintain his sentencing requirements. When we came to talk about the requirement that he attend the language and culture centre, Monti said: "I'm looking forward to that." He went on to explain that, although he was not Gumbaynggirr, his two children were. "It will be good to be able to teach and learn with my kids," he commented.

Monti was seeing an opportunity. It was an opportunity born of adversity.

Sometimes in life things do not seem to be going our way. Nothing seems to work. We become ill, lose a lot of money, our relationship ends, or we are made redundant. The future can look hopeless or bleak. We may want to give up or turn to inappropriate props such as alcohol, drugs or crime. Yet, as Monti found, an opportunity may be lying dormant within the adversity.

However, an opportunity does not grab us; we have to look for it, then we have to grab it. Monti could have undertaken the language and culture course because he had to, perhaps resenting

---

[33] Gumbaynggirr is the local tribal grouping in the area and is the language of the local indigenous culture.

every lesson. But he didn't. In the adversity Monti saw the opportunity and grabbed it.

Trauma can be considered as an extreme form of adversity. Interestingly, some research shows that almost three-quarters of people who survive a traumatic experience come through that experience with positive psychological benefits, including greater creative insight. Of course, this is not to suggest that you go out and deliberately provoke a traumatic experience because it may lead to creative insight. What it does show, however, is that we can find opportunities everywhere, even in the places we would least expect.

Missed Opportunities

I mentioned earlier that if we remain closed we will miss opportunities. We close ourselves off to opportunities in many ways, but at the heart of many of these ways is that of hanging on to our inherited, constructed or borrowed ideas of what the solutions should be. In simple terms, we cling to ideologies. An ideology is simply a connected set of beliefs about how things should be and the methods by which they can be obtained. It is possible to have political ideologies, religious ideologies, social ideologies. We can have psychological ideologies, or human or community development ideologies. Ideologies come in a wide variety of guises: socialism, capitalism, liberalism, progressive, republican, democrat are just some of the "big" political ideologies. We can also hold onto what could be called "small" ideologies, e.g. fight fire with fire, or turn the other cheek are two that represent conflicting ideas of how to solve conflict.

When South Africa began to dismantle the apartheid system in the early 1990s, many around the world feared that the nation would descend into a bloodbath, with native Africans out for revenge, and white settlers taking up arms to protect what they saw as theirs. The prevailing ideological solution within much of Africa at the time was to use African values, a set of undefined values that many African rulers claimed meant solidarity against the west. But, Nelson Mandela, newly freed after 27 years imprisoned by the apartheid state, said "no." Mandela espoused values of human rights, democracy and freedom of speech. He did not want to be trapped in the ideology that was prevalent at the time throughout the continent. Mandela also had the historic model of the Nuremberg Trials as an example of achieving justice – retributive justice (the predominant model of state justice systems worldwide). Many western leaders exhorted him to use this mode. Mandela could have clung to the African values ideology or he could have been swayed by the retributive justice ideology. Instead, he remained open to opportunities. He proposed something radically different to either of these approaches.

The Truth and Reconciliation Commission that he set up sought to find a new solution. Mandela appointed Bishop Desmond Tutu (an outspoken Anglican cleric of the apartheid system) to be the Chairman. Bishop Tutu describes what happened:[34] *"When, at last, our leaders were released from prison, it was feared that our transition to democracy would become a bloodbath of revenge and retaliation. Miraculously we chose another future. We chose forgiveness. At the time, we knew that telling the truth and healing our history was the only way to save our country from certain destruction. We did not know where this choice would lead us. The process we embarked on through the Truth and Reconciliation Commission was, as all real growth proves to be, astoundingly painful and profoundly beautiful."*

Nelson Mandela, Bishop Tutu, and many others decided not to blinker themselves with ideology. By not doing so, they were able to discover and explore another opportunity.

We too can very easily miss opportunities because of our entrenched views and positions. Even the community development worker can be caught in this trap by hanging onto a particular model of community development (e.g. social justice model, ecological model, social engagement, capacity development).

When we come across a new idea that does not fit our ideological views, then one option is to reject it because it does not conform to how we think the world should be or the method by which

---

[34] Tutu, Desmond & Tutu, Mpho. 2014

our view of the world should be achieved. That is a mistake. It is a trap. We enter the trap simply by being unwilling to consider any other method than those that fit within our ideology. In many ways our ideology has become our comfort zone. We need to be able to step beyond that comfort zone in order to recognise the opportunity that lies outside.

The above should not be read as suggesting that all models, worldviews or ideologies need be rejected. To begin with, it is not possible to do so. We construct our view of reality in our minds, and that allows us to operate in the world. In order to not miss opportunities, though, we need to hold our views and ideologies lightly. We cannot allow them to define us. Here's a question that you might like to consider: how many opportunities have you missed because of clinging to a particular ideology or perception of the world?

VIII
FLOW

Have you ever sat down with someone you have just met and found that the conversation just seems to flow? There is almost no conscious effort required. There are no awkward silences or "ums" and "ahs." You sit together talking and then find that an hour or two hours have passed by without you noticing. You and your new acquaintance have just gone with the flow.

When that sort of dialogue takes place, the creative opportunities just flow from the conversation. Indeed, more opportunities may appear than we can consciously capture and record. Of course, this flowing conversation takes place because the environment within which it occurs is a nurturing, encouraging one. Nurture and encouragement are considered in Chapter XII – Encouraging.

For the time being, I will concentrate on the topic of flow and tease out what it may mean for emergence.

"Go with the flow" is an often heard refrain, but what does it mean in the context of this inquiry? Firstly, let me make it very clear that I am not advocating fatalism or a sense of sitting back and seeing where the flow takes us. Definitely not. I am seeking a more active role for those of us involved in community development, social justice, and sustainability. Rather, the idea is more one of using the energy that exists in positive, worthwhile ways rather than vainly fighting against the energy.

A kayaker knows this principle well. It is far easier to use the flow of a river to your advantage than it is to battle against the current. However, the kayaker is not inactive in this endeavour. If the kayak is not actively kept in the flow of the current then the kayak can very easily end up sidelong to the flow, often meaning that the kayaker goes for a swim (unless they are adept at the Eskimo Roll technique) or the kayak gets smashed into rocks. Often an inexperienced kayaker, when first encountering rapids, will stop paddling. They then find that the river has taken control, forced them sideways and suddenly they are upside down. An experienced kayaker, however, when entering a section of rapids, will maintain their paddle stroke, sometimes even upping the tempo. They know that by maintaining the momentum of the kayak they can remain upright and in the flow of the river.

To continue with the metaphor of the kayaker, here's a little more. When a kayaker enters a river they usually have a goal of some sort. It may be getting to a point further down the river. In the South Island of New Zealand there is a well-known multisport race (the Coast-to-Coast) that has a kayak leg that involves paddling a 67 km section of a rapidly flowing, often turbulent river known as the Waimakariri. I raced in this event a few times and each time I got into my kayak I would have a goal of getting to the end of that 67 km. However, although I had that goal, I had to bring myself to the present moment in the flow of the river and be aware of my paddle technique and my body posture. I had to watch out for the tell-tale signs of rocks, look out for eddies and check the actions and manoeuvres of other kayakers around me. I had my goals, but to get to them I had to concentrate on the flow that I was in right now. There was no sitting back and just drifting, that would have had me upside down or smashed against a rock before I'd gone too far. I used the flow, I didn't allow it to use me, nor did I try to control the flow. That is the difference that we are looking for in the context of this acronym.

Martial arts practitioners also understand the meaning of flow: recognising that the energy of an opponent can often be used against them, rather than having to directly resist the opponent. To the martial arts practitioner, flow is also contrasted with methods that advocate a step-by-step mechanistic approach.

Flow cannot be contained by a structure or prescribed form. It cannot be described by a 1-2-3-step-1-2-3-step... process. It just flows. Watch a stream closely for long enough and you will notice that the water does not flow past you in a uniform manner. It undulates, swirls, contains micro-eddies. In keeping with one of the themes of this book, it flows chaotically.

When creative opportunities flow from our encouraging encounters then that is exactly how we need to deal with them. As soon as we try to stem the flow, or direct it on a predetermined path, then we have lost the opportunity. When we try to control the thoughts and ideas of those we are interacting with, then we are no longer encouraging them and we have lost the opportunity.

To remain with the flow we have to give up one of our most cherished yearnings – the yearning for control.

Humanity's desire for control could quite possibly qualify as the single most damaging cause of the emergencies facing us. Think of it for a minute. Why do we suffer wars and terrorism? Someone wants to subjugate or *control* someone else, or one nation wants to *control* the land or resources of another. Why does inequality exist? One sector of society wants to *control* more and more of the total wealth and income. Why are we facing biodiversity loss? Agribusiness and transnationals want to *control* the production and distribution of food and other resources. Why does corruption in our legislatures occur? Some politicians want to *control* who has access to power and who does not.

The replies given to each of the above questions are obviously short and do not provide a fully expounded answer, however, it is hard to argue anything other than that the desire for control is at the base of many of the issues facing us.

The yearning for control is closely associated with the slogan "the end justifies the means." If we desire a particular outcome (end), then this slogan suggests that we can control other people, the environment or resources however we wish, in order to achieve that end. But, ends and means are not separate entities, they are intimately intertwined. Joanna Macy[35] defines means as *"ends in the making."*

---

[35] Joanna Macy is an American deep ecologist, engaged Buddhist and systems thinker who has written extensively on environmental issues, nuclear weapons disarmament and personal empowerment.

Many of those working in the fields of social justice, community development, and sustainability recognise the truth of Macy's words. What needs to be appreciated further in the present context is that when we are searching for collective responses to the emergencies, we must give up our wish to control the outcome, or sometimes even the process, of the dialogue. That means going with the flow. It means having and expressing our opinions, our thoughts and our ideas, but it also means listening to those of others and being open to accepting other perspectives and possibly even dispensing with our own. It means not always being right and it means having the courage to recognise that. As the American rock musician, Frank Zappa, so famously quipped: *"The mind is like a parachute. It doesn't work if it is not open."*

Allowing dialogue and actions to flow does not mean that we will always be heading in the direction that we want to go, or towards the solutions we desire. To return to the metaphor of the river and the kayaker; occasionally we will get caught up in eddies, whirlpools or cataracts. Fighting these, any kayaker will tell you, often ends in disaster.

Eddies, whirlpools, and cataracts may turn out to be signs that we need to slow down. Perhaps some members of our group or organisation are struggling to keep up with the new ideas or new ways of doing something. We need to stop and nurture our colleagues. Perhaps there are factors that we hadn't sufficiently considered. Maybe we need to return to a previous stage in our thinking. Maybe we hadn't consulted adequately with one group of people. Perhaps a previously unknown piece of information comes to our attention that changes how we look at an issue.

Fighting the eddies, whirlpools, and cataracts within organisations and communities is likely to end in collective folly – the exact opposite of collective wisdom. Collective folly is like the sly fox that covers itself in sheep's clothing. Outwardly it can appear that our organisation has unity or agreement in our deliberations or intended actions. Yet, underneath that veneer of harmony lies uncertainty, disagreement, or even hostility. How does this happen?

We become overly focused on the outcome and neglect the hesitancy of members of the group. In our rush towards consensus, full agreement, or concord, the group can easily ignore some members, actively argue against others, or simply not encourage those who are quiet. Yet, it may be that those who are hesitant may be holding on to a vital bit of information or insight, and they may not even realise it. Instead of offering their uncertainty up to the group, these group members may remain quiet for fear of blocking what appears to be universal agreement, or from fear of being ridiculed.

The authors of *The Power of Collective Wisdom; and the trap of collective folly* provide a tragic example of collective folly at work.[36] In early 1986 NASA was preparing to launch the Space Shuttle Challenger, with seven crew, into space. The day before the launch was scheduled one of the engineers with one of the contractors to the program recommended to NASA officials that the launch be cancelled. The engineer had doubts over the efficacy of O-ring seals on the Challenger if the launch proceeded in cold conditions (as was forecast). NASA had already delayed the launch four times and was reluctant to do so again because of data that even the contractor's engineers admitted was not definitive. However, the engineers were hesitant and were concerned that a launch under the circumstances could result in failure.

During a conference call between NASA and the contractor, between management and engineers, a senior manager for the contractor requested that they go off-line to enable the contractor to take another look at their recommendation. During the course of the discussion by the contractors, the general manager said: "we have to make a management decision." A vote was held, but it involved managers only, not the engineers. The vote was unanimous – to proceed with the launch.

It is now graphic history as to what happened. Seventy-three seconds after the launch, the Challenger exploded killing all seven

---

[36] Briskin, Erickson, Ott & Callanan, 2009.

astronauts on board. The images of that explosion were broadcast on television worldwide.

It is a chilling and tragic warning of the perils of ignoring the eddies, whirlpools, and cataracts in the flow. NASA wanted a launch. The managers at the contracting firm wanted to maintain their agreement with NASA. The launch went ahead. The engineers were initially listened to, but their concerns were ignored, and they were barred from the final decision-making.

We can all do that. We can all be part of groups, communities, and nations where the desire to advance our objectives and to maintain a sense of unity can end in disaster.

Of course, it is not always like that, thankfully. Groups, communities and even nations can work within the flow and achieve a collective wisdom. Remaining true to the flow, eddies and all, allows us to follow a wise current.

When a discussion or group activity is in flow we get a sense of freedom, a sense that everything is just right, that we don't have to expend too much energy. When we get those feelings then we can be assured that we may be on the right track, that what we are doing is correct, appropriate and emergent.

Paradoxically, when we are in the flow it can feel as if we are not really doing anything, yet things happen. In Taoism this idea is encapsulated in the concept of wu wei. Wu wei can be translated as the "action of non-action." To our western ears that can sound nonsensical. However, remember that we in the west have lived for centuries with a cultural belief that says actions happen in linear fashion and that doing one thing causes something else to happen – although theories such as Chaos Theory are challenging that notion. So, to our ears, how is it possible that something can happen through non-action? Yet, that is exactly what happens when we get into flow, or as many athletes call it, "enter the zone."

In western society, the greatest contributor to the study of flow is the Hungarian psychologist Mihaly Csikszentmihalyi (presently Professor of Psychology and Management at Claremont Graduate University in California.) Csikszentmihalyi has published many books on flow, creativity, and happiness. From his studies of flow he notes that no matter what the flow experience was, nor what triggered it, all flow experiences have in common that they *"provided a sense of discovery, a creative feeling of transporting the person into a new reality. It pushed the person to higher levels of performance and led to previously undreamed-of states of consciousness. In short, it transformed the self by making it more complex."[37]*

Csikszentmihalyi uses a diagram (see below) to explain how and why this occurs. When our skill level and the challenges we face are in alignment then we experience flow. If however, the challenges we face are greater than our skills, we can suffer from anxiety. On the other hand, when the challenges presented to us are well below our skill level, boredom sets in.

If we are finding ourselves anxious, as we would be at the point "A" in the diagram, the way to get back into the flow channel is to increase our skills. Should it be boredom we are suffering from (position "B" in the diagram) then we need to up our challenges in order to get back into the flow channel.

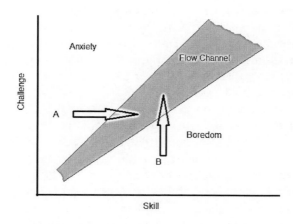

[37] Csikszentmihalyi, Mihaly. 1990.

In addition to boredom and anxiety, Csikszentmihalyi added the state of apathy, which can be thought of as a combination of low skill and low challenge – the zone in the bottom left corner of the diagram.

Fortunately for us, Csikszentmihalyi did not stop at describing the effects of flow but went on to discuss the conditions that enable us to be in flow. One of these conditions is the extent to which we are able to organise our consciousness so that we enter into an activity or situation for its own sake rather than for the benefits that we may get from it. Think of a game of tennis. If we play the game for its own sake, for the enjoyment of it, then we are likely to enter into a state of flow. However, if we play the game with the intent of "smashing the other person out of the court" then we are less likely to enjoy a state of flow, at least not continuously. We may thoroughly enjoy the first time we win, but if we remain in that state of consciousness, then the next game (or others to come) are unlikely to be as enjoyable.

But doesn't this negate the flow state of athletes who "enter the zone?" No, it doesn't. Those athletes who get into the zone often find themselves not thinking at all about whether they are winning or losing, but rather are directing their mental energies towards their technique, the state of their body and the immediate flight of the ball. Having been a competitive runner for over 40 years, I know that some of my best races came when I was in the zone that had me thinking about stride length, hurdling technique, relaxation, breathing, and less to do with being concerned to beat a fellow competitor, or about the ultimate outcome of the race.

The same is true in the context of the **COFFEE** concept. We can enter into an encouraging encounter for its own sake, without thinking that we have a particular outcome to achieve. When we do so, we enter into flow and find, as if by magic, that creative opportunities emerge from that encounter.

What restricts our ability to organise our consciousness in ways that enable flow to occur? Csikszentmihalyi notes that if we are either overly self-conscious or excessively self-centred then we will have difficulty experiencing flow. The self-conscious person is unable to enter flow conditions because of fearing how others will perceive them, or of creating the wrong impression. A self-centred person is the opposite. A self-centred person is unable to experience flow because they enter the situation only on the basis of how the situation can benefit them, and hence are unable to connect with the fluidity of the situation.

Both the self-conscious person and the self-centred person are too much focused on themselves (either worried about what others think of them or having no regard to others) to have any energy left over to enjoy the situation for its own sake – the state of flow. It should be noted here that self-centredness is not the same as being aware of one's state. Being aware of our breathing, our relaxation, or our concentration is not the same as being self-centred. Self-centredness is where we believe ourselves to be the centre of things and the outcomes of the situation are for our own personal benefit.

Overcoming these two states (self-consciousness and self-centredness) should come fairly easily to most people working in community development and/or social justice. After all, to work in these areas requires a compassionate and empathic approach to working with others. Those working in these areas often also bring a curiosity to their work, and this trait appears to be characteristic of a flowing state.

To summarise; we can enter a state of flow if we bring some, or all, of the following qualities into our encounters:

- Entering the activity or situation for its own sake,
- Enjoying the interplay between the participants in the activity or situation,
- Bringing a sense of curiosity and wonder to the encounter,
- Recognising the uniqueness of others involved; their skills, knowledge, and wisdom,
- Overcoming our desire for control over the final outcome,
- Being open to the turbulence and fluctuations that occur along the way, and
- Focusing on the present, the now.

IX
FROM

From whence do our solutions to our multi-faceted emergency stem? If we do not trust our leaders and politicians to make the right decisions then where do we look for guidance, leadership or action? This book argues that the ideas, the solutions, and the actions begin with and flow from all of us, from communities and the collective knowledge, experience, skills and wisdom that they contain.

This approach turns on its head the classic western notion of development. The classic western approach is one in which experts enter a community or nation, assess the needs and then design a program or infrastructure to address those needs. Classically there was little consultation with the local community and even less of an attempt to involve the community in the design of any program or intervention. Often this approach led to the program eventually collapsing or the infrastructure being under-utilised. Many times this collapse could be attributed to the "experts" incorrectly identifying the needs or the problem, let alone the solution.

But, when the process begins with and flows from within communities, then the chances of correctly identifying the issues and then designing the appropriate response are greatly enhanced.

This approach emphasises that power and decision-making shift from the top to the bottom, from the centre to the margins, and from hierarchies to interconnected networks. It puts connected communities firmly in the role of decision-makers and implementers of policy.

"But what if local communities do not have the knowledge, or skills necessary?" is a common argument raised against allowing ordinary citizens, the man and woman in the street - "commoners" - to become decision-makers. This quarrel is based on prejudice and misinformation. The prejudice is that only those with expertise are in the best position to make decisions. The misinformation is that the rest of us have no knowledge or wisdom worthy of bringing to the table. The arguments are all bound up in the notions of expertise and wisdom.

Expertise and Wisdom

Let us consider the prejudice first. The "expert" may come in various guises: community health expert, education expert, city planning expert, even the community development or social justice expert. In each case, the expert may have some useful expertise to offer, but that does not make them the best decision-maker in any community setting. Indeed, an expert in a decision-making role can be disastrous.

A 2006 study found that the more power an individual has or claims to have, the more likely they are to over-value their own viewpoint and are less capable of considering another person's perspective.[38] The same researcher, in 2012, noted that those with a sense of power were often over-confident in their decision-making.[39]

Remember too, that becoming an expert in a subject usually involves knowing more and more about a topic that is more and more specialised. In short: knowing more and more about less and less. Our world is a complex, interconnected and diverse one. We, and it, contain contradictions, anomalies, and inconsistencies. In such a world our decision-making processes must ensure that a wide variety of perspectives and ideas are taken into account. The expert has a place in that, but only one place of many.

It is of little benefit if a decision made by an expert is the *right* one in their view if it does not make *sense* to those on whom the decision is imposed.

Look around the world. Often, where we see conflict, bitterness or social isolation, we will also find that a decision has been imposed by someone (or a group) who have done so in the belief that

---

[38] Galinsky, Adam et al. 2006.
[39] Galinsky, Adam et al. March 2012.

theirs was the correct one to make. That applies just as much to a local neighbourhood as it does to international conflict.

The tower block building projects that began in the 1950s in England are a case in point. Architects and city planners in England embraced with zeal the ideas of architects such as Le Corbusier and Walter Gropius who became known for their minimalist approach. Le Corbusier's idea was magnified from the simple stripped down villa into stack upon stack of bare, uniform multi-storied dwellings. Town planning experts and architectural experts embraced the idea with glee, but no-one bothered to ask the potential inhabitants.

Within just a few years the cracks were appearing, not only in the buildings themselves but also in the social fabric. In May 1968 Ronan Point, a 22 storey tower block in East London, partially collapsed killing 4 people and injuring 17. It wasn't the only one.

But it was the tearing apart of social cohesion that was perhaps the biggest failing of this expert-driven approach to housing. The adults living in these towers experienced high rates of stress, mental health problems, and marriage breakdown. Their children fared no better. Tower-rise children had high rates of hyperactivity and were prone to greater levels of hostility and juvenile delinquency (even when socio-economic status was adjusted for) than that of the general population.

Even though much is known about the damage to social infrastructure that these towers create, they are still being built. There are many commentators and community workers in England who are now advocating for a return to the terraced housing style that England is so well known for.

So, beware the expert, but do not ignore the expert. They can have useful information or knowledge, but it does not make them the best decision-maker.

Now to the misinformation: that the common person has nothing of value to bring to the table. Looked at on an individual basis that may be partially valid, but when we bring common people, everyday citizens, together we find that something amazing happens -- wisdom emerges.

Over 100 years ago an English statistician and hereditary scientist, Francis Galton, walked to his local county fair. Galton, then in his 80s, had spent his life attempting to prove that most people did not have enough intelligence to lead society. Wandering around the fair he came across a competition to guess the weight of an ox. Amongst the entrants, there were a few cattle breeders, butchers, and farmers who, Galton surmised, would be expert enough to guess fairly accurately the weight of the ox. However, most of the almost 800 punters were common folk, with no apparent expertise in ox-weighing. After the competition had ended and the prize-winner announced, Galton obtained all the winning entries from the organisers.

Being the statistician that he was, Galton calculated the average guessed weight. Before doing so, Galton hypothesised that this average guess would be a long way from the true weight because most of the punters were non-experts. However, what Galton discovered staggered him and challenged him to re-think his ideas about expertise and "common" knowledge. The true weight of the ox was 1,198 pounds – the average vote turned out to be 1,197 pounds. This average was closer than that of any of the individual "experts" who had entered the competition.

On that day in Plymouth, 1906, Galton discovered what has since come to be known as "the wisdom of crowds." Since Galton's time, many researchers and activists have sought to discover what can happen when a group of ordinary, common people are brought together for some specific purpose. These activities and experiments have suggested that Galton had only scratched the surface of the "wisdom of crowds" phenomenon. Galton had observed only what happened when a number of individuals put their guesses into a hat and the average was calculated. Instances since then have noted that when individuals come together collectively to discuss, to listen to others, and then come to considered, mutually agreed outcomes the results can be exceptional. Galton's experiment involved a non-complex situation - an average of individual votes was sufficient for his purposes. But, when we are dealing with complexity we need much more than an agglomeration of individual, non-reflective, responses – we need dialogue. And dialogue is at the heart of the wisdom of crowds.

The Wisdom of Crowds, or Collective Wisdom as it has come to be known today, has been defined as a *"capacity to learn together and evolve toward something greater and wiser than what we can do as individuals alone… Collective wisdom is a deepening of collective understanding; it is a way we can come together to address our social world and the need for its repair."*[40]

The power of collective wisdom is that it comes from all of us. Wisdom is not limited to the expert or those in authority; wisdom is something that we can collectively attain.

The discerning reader will have noticed that the title of the book just quoted includes the phrase *"and the trap of collective folly."* This is an important point. Not all crowds or groupings of people arrive at wise decisions. It is quite easy for groups to be led into fallacious, foolish or downright dangerous areas. Another writer on the subject has suggested four elements that are necessary in group settings to enable a wise, as opposed to foolish, decision to emerge. James Surowiecki[41] identifies these four elements:

- Diversity of opinion.
- Independence, so that each person's opinions are not determined by others in the group. In other words, group or cultural norms can be overcome, and people are not coerced into holding a particular viewpoint.
- Decentralisation. Local knowledge is identified and valued.
- Aggregation. A method or technique is applied that enables the private ideas, thoughts, and wisdom of people to merge into a collective decision.

It is from such groups that wisdom can emerge. An initiative in Canada in 1991 demonstrated that when Surowiecki's elements are

---

[40] Briskin, Erickson, Ott & Callanan, 2009.
[41] Surowiecki, James. 2004.

brought together, the wisdom of a diverse group of people can be remarkable.

The *People's Verdict* was sponsored by Macleans (the national weekly current affairs magazine in Canada). Macleans brought together 12 randomly selected Canadians for three days of dialogue and decision-making. Knowing nothing of each other, and coming from a diverse background with differing views, they were given the task of coming up with a vision for the future of Canada. Included amongst the 12 were Quebec separatists, federalists, a native Canadian and other seemingly disparate viewpoints. Macleans was so impressed with the exercise that it devoted its entire 1 July 1991 edition to an explanation of the process, the participants, and the outcome. The final document covered a raft of issues from education to the economy, from individual rights to government and the Constitution. Notwithstanding their prior differences and backgrounds, all 12 participants enthusiastically signed the document.[42]

But it wasn't just what the 12 Canadians produced that so impressed Macleans. As the Editor (Kevin Doyle) noted in his editorial, *"...one of the most striking elements of the remarkable weekend was the sheer strength of the emotional attachment that the participants showed for Canada—either Canada as it is or a Canada that could be."*

The Macleans experiment showed that it is possible to bring together ordinary people, with disparate views and backgrounds, and through a facilitated process of analysis and dialogue, put aside their differences and come to a consensus over the final outcome.

Many of the emergencies and other issues facing us are either recent phenomena or they are now so interwoven with other issues that complexity compels us to look for solutions that we have never thought of before. Earlier in this book I quoted Einstein, it is worth

---

[42] For a more comprehensive outline of the process, participants, and outcome see this webpage from the *Co-intelligence Institute*: http://www.co-intelligence.org/S-Canadaadvrsariesdream.html Accessed 10 July 2016

repeating the quote: *"We can't solve problems using the same thinking we used when we created them."*

So, if we haven't thought of them before, and we need to use different thinking to what we have always used, where do these new ideas come from? If, as Einstein (and indeed, others[43]) suggest, we need to use different thinking then we must be prepared to let go of the thinking patterns that we have become used to.

This is not easy to do. Individually, we have been conditioned from birth to think in particular styles, to assume that the way we *think* the world works *is* the way the world works. Socially and culturally this conditioning and assumed knowledge of the world has been with us for centuries, possibly millennia.

In that previous paragraph I used the phrase "the way we think the world works." I could have used the phrase "the way we believe the world works." Because, ultimately, our thoughts and what we think are often manifestations of our belief system. We can have different beliefs, such as belief in ghosts, belief that JF Kennedy was killed by the mafia or a belief that the world will end tomorrow. A belief system, however, is something more than a non-related jumble of beliefs. A belief system is exactly as it sounds – a system of mutually supporting beliefs that guide our lives, almost from the time we wake in the morning until the time we fall asleep in the evening.

Belief systems can be informed by scientific, religious, philosophical, and other outlooks on the world. With most of these belief systems we can identify the various beliefs that make up the system, we can shine a torch of inquiry upon them. We can question our belief system, and may even discard one belief system to replace it with another. Historically we discarded the belief system that the sun revolved around the earth in favour of the heliocentric system. Individually we may move from one religious belief system to another.

---

[43] e.g. E.F. Schumacher, Joanna Macy, David Suzuki, Dalai Lama, Pope Francis, Xiuhtezcatl Martinez (young teenage founder of *Earth Guardians*) and many others.

But there is one belief system that we often are not aware of – our culture. Each of us lives in and are an intimate part of, a culture. Culture is based on a belief system. Admittedly it is a deeply ingrained belief system, so ingrained that we find it difficult to explain what culture is. If asked, we might point to music, dance, architecture, or fashion. We might even find it so difficult that we say "we don't have a culture," and point to indigenous people, or some other group and say "they have culture." It has been said that asking someone to describe their culture is like asking a fish to describe water. Culture is all around us, it passes through us, it is always there, and hence we don't notice it. Culture has been likened to an iceberg, where just 10% of it is above the surface, and visible. The visible signs of culture include such things as food, dance, language, arts and crafts, flags, and holidays.

The 90% that is below the surface and is mostly invisible includes how we raise children, our attitude to elders, decision-making practices, manners, and our notions of right and wrong. See the diagram for a fuller (but even then, non-exhaustive) list.

Our culture provides us with the beliefs that allow us to think of how the world works. And that is why it is so difficult for us to let go of how we think/believe the world works. Letting go of thinking patterns

Dance   Literature
Art   Food   Language
Dress   Music   Flags
Festivals and Holidays

Communication styles
Eye contact   Body language
Concepts of Beauty   Manners   Time
Leadership styles   Concept of self
Authority   Marriage   Personal space
Sex   Raising children   Eldership
Work habits   Justice   Fairness
Cooperation and competition   Aging
Family   Sin
Decision-making
Male/female roles ,,,,,,,,,,

that have been influenced by our cultural belief system is extremely difficult to do, simply because we often do not see the underlying beliefs of our culture.

Letting go and shifting our consciousness requires effort that is rooted in non-effort. That sounds contradictory, perhaps even foolish. So, let me explain.

We all know that letting go of something is scary. Whether it be as a child letting go of a swinging rope as it passes over a pond or river so that we drop into the water, or letting go of a relationship that has become unhealthy. It is frightening going into the unknown. We have to make the effort to let go. But then, when we do let go, it is effortless and we pass through an empty space before we arrive at the new place.

Indeed, it is this emptiness that we need in order to discover new ways of thinking and creating. Let me make a bit more use of the coffee analogy. Think of an empty coffee cup. Pick up one now and look at it. You can touch it, see it, and describe it. It's likely to be round with a handle on one side, made of pottery, plastic, tin, or some other material. But, what is it that allows the coffee to be smelt and tasted? The space, the empty space. If there was no empty space then where would the coffee go?

It is the same with discovering where our new thinking can come from. It comes from an empty space. The Buddhist term *shunyata* is worth exploring in this context. *Shunyata* has often been translated as empty, yet the term has a far more expansive meaning than that. The Buddhist scholar, David Loy describes it this way:[44] *"It comes from the root* shunya, *which means 'to swell' in two senses: hollow or empty, and also like the womb of a pregnant woman."*

Loy notes that the second meaning implies a "fullness and limitless possibility." In many senses this limitless possibility is what is meant by the first two words in the **COFFEE** acronym: creative opportunity.

---

[44] Loy, David. 1998.

If we allow that emptiness to arise in our consciousness, then we will find that we have the space for new thinking; new ways of seeing the world can emerge. How do we do that?

The classic answer, of course, is meditation. Clearing the mind of its clutter, clatter and chatter is one of the benefits of meditation. The Buddhists have a name for this cluttered and chattering mind. They call it *Monkey Mind* – meaning a mind that is unsettled, rambling, uncontrollable, capricious, restless, confused and other similar concepts.

Research at Yale University in 2011 *"found that the main nodes of the default-mode network (medial prefrontal and posterior cingulate cortices) were relatively deactivated in experienced meditators across all meditation types."*[45] What? That's the academic phrasing. What does it mean in everyday English? Here's my interpretation: Most of the time the networks in the human brain responsible for wandering thoughts are switched to the "on" position. However, with meditation, this default position can be switched to "off."

Another study, this time at the University of California at Santa Barbara, found that after just two weeks of meditation training participants had significantly increased focus and memory capability.[46]

These two studies are only two amongst dozens of pieces of research into the benefits of meditation. Besides the benefits of increased awareness, concentration, attention, and memory that are pertinent here, there are a number of other benefits that have also received scientific attention. Included amongst these are: reduction in depression and anxiety, longer lived brain grey matter, easing of addictions, healthier immune systems, higher levels of productivity, and a more positive outlook on life.

---

[45] Brewer, Worhunsky, Gray, Tang, Weber & Kober, 13 Dec 2011, Vol 108, No 50, pp 20254-20259
[46] Mrazek, Franklin, Phillips, Baird & Schooler, May 2013, pp 776-781

This book is not going to offer advice or techniques on meditation – there are numerous sources available for the reader who may be interested.

In the context of this book, we are interested in settling our mind, emptying it if you will, to allow new thinking to emerge. When we sit with another person, one way that we can empty our mind is to dispense with any prejudice, assumptions or pre-prepared conclusions that we may bring to the dialogue. If we are able to truly listen to other people, without interruption, without comment, without analysis, and without judgment, then we have a chance to empty our mind to an extent where we may find that new thinking emerges.

That's what I mean when I say it is effortless. We don't have to do anything. We just listen. Yet, it is a type of listening that in our everyday lives is uncommon. I shall have more to say on the topic of listening in the next section (See pp 95-98). For now, it is important to recognise that where our creative opportunities come from is from finding a space in which new thinking can emerge. That space is created by dispensing with our old habits, beliefs, judgments and assumptions. That space is created by allowing our minds to settle. Whether it is by meditation, listening to waves breaking on a shore or going for a walk amongst trees, we can all find a way. That space is also created by actively encouraging and creatively listening to those with whom we are engaged. Which brings us to...

X
ENCOURAGING

How many of us respond well to encouragement? Most of us, when appreciated, commended, or acknowledged, operate at a higher level and respond with enthusiasm, confidence, and creativity. As long ago as 1949, a social researcher asked employees to rank the rewards of their jobs. Number one on the list was "feeling appreciated," ranking higher even than the incentive that is often assumed to be the main motivating factor – money.

Most of us too, when in conversation with someone, will find the conversation stimulating and rewarding when we feel respected, acknowledged and listened to. It matters little whether the conversation is between just two people, or whether we are in a workshop or seminar setting where there may be 200 or more people present.

What is involved when we encourage (literally *hearten*[47]) someone? When I have asked people to brainstorm words associated with encourage these are some of the words that are mentioned: trust, listening, acknowledgement, helping, supporting, praising, being present, guiding, suspending judgment, empathy, and sympathy.

Let us look at five of those notions as they, perhaps more than the others, encapsulate all the rest when we look at them closely. These five are: empathy, trust, listening (and speaking, being present, and suspending judgment. Following these five notions, I shall then look at some other ways in which we can be encouraging.

Empathy

The author of *The 7 Habits of Highly Effective People*, Stephen Covey,[48] connected empathy with the ability to creatively

---

[47] Encourage comes from Old French, *en* meaning "make, put in" and *corage* – heart.
[48] Covey, Stephen R. 1989

solve problems. The highly influential author, educator and motivational speaker noted that *"When you show deep empathy toward others, their defensive energy goes down, and positive energy replaces it. That's when you can get more creative in solving problems."*

Empathy has a close cousin, sympathy, and both derive from the same root word – *pathos*. *Pathos* is a Greek word that can be translated as suffering, feeling, emotion or calamity. Literally, it means what befalls one. Sympathy is obtained by adding the prefix *sym* which has the meaning of *together* or *with*. Empathy adds the prefix *em* meaning *in*. The subtle difference in the two words can be understood from this. Sympathy is a feeling of caring for or understanding the suffering of others. Empathy, on the other hand, goes deeper and is the ability to experience the suffering of others. Empathy allows us to understand what others are feeling either because we have experienced similar feelings or have the ability to step out of our own experience and discover the feelings that the other person or persons are undergoing. Psychologically, empathy and sympathy have been distinguished from each other since 1987 when two psychologists (Nancy Eisenberg and Janet Strayer) defined empathy as "emotional matching" and sympathy as "sorrow or concern for another's welfare."[49]

The word empathy itself is a fairly recent immigrant to the English language. In 1909 it was translated from the German word *Einfühling* (in-feeling). It was to be over one hundred years before the neuroscience of empathy was revealed. Californian neurophysiologists identified what are known as mirror neurons in the human brain.[50] These neurons effectively mirror in our brain what is happening emotionally for another person. Via this mechanism, our brains react as if what we are seeing or hearing from another person is actually happening to ourselves, within our own bodies.

---

[49] Nancy Eisenberg (Arizona State University) & Janet Strayer (Simon Fraser University), *Empathy and its development*, Cambridge University Press, 1987.
[50] Quoted in Klein, Stefan. 2014

Fortunately, our mirror neurons don't confine themselves just to feelings of suffering. When others are happy, joyful, or having fun, we can feel those emotions also via our mirror neurons. We have the capacity to feel empathetic towards someone experiencing ecstasy just as easily as we can towards someone in pain.

Although we may have mirror neurons and hence the ability to be empathetic, that does not mean that we are automatically highly skilled empathic people. We are able to increase our ability to empathise. Neuroscientists are discovering that the brain has the ability to adapt and change its neuro-pathways. Neuroplasticity is a very recent science, but already the findings from that science have radical implications for the way we relate to one another. One of those implications is that we can learn to become better empathisers. We can improve our empathy quotient if you like.[51]

In order to be able to empathise with someone else, we must be able to identify with our own feelings and emotions. The more self-aware we are the better we are at empathising with others.[52] Thus to be able to outwardly empathise we need to inwardly become attuned to our own feelings and emotions. When we can better understand and identify our own feelings and emotions then we become better empathisers. It may be true to say that women are generally better able to do this than men, but all of us are able to learn the language of feelings and emotions. Generally speaking, men are not taught this language. Indeed, in western culture men have been dis-encouraged to learn the language, and actively admonished for speaking it. How many men who are reading this will remember being told as boys that "big boys don't cry" or "harden up and take it like a man"? Men are supposed to be stoic and able to contain their feelings inside and not show them publicly. But, all is not lost. Like any language, the language of feelings and emotions can be learnt - very easily too - because often we already know the vocabulary. We

---

[51] In fact an Empathy Quotient (EQ) has been developed at the Autism Research Centre at the University of Cambridge.
[52] Goleman, Daniel. 1996

know what words like sad, disheartened, irritated, joyous, excited, and dozens more mean. We just need to learn how to use them.

Knowing the words is one thing, speaking them is another, and recognising the feeling is something else again. Being comfortable with our feelings and being comfortable expressing them is crucial to being able to empathise. Learning to expand our feeling vocabulary helps us discover the nuances of our feelings, giving us greater insight into our own emotions as well as enhancing our ability to recognise the feelings displayed by others. There are dozens of feeling lists available on the internet, and even a feeling wheel that enables us to begin with a feeling that is close to what we are experiencing, but not quite right. From that close feeling we move out to the next rim of the wheel and eventually arrive at a word that describes exactly what we are feeling. In this way, we can hone not only our language but also our feelings. (See Kaitlin Robb's Feeling Wheel below)

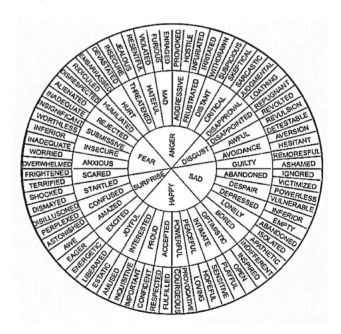

How else might we develop our empathy? Roman Krznaric, the cultural thinker/writer, and founder of the world's first Empathy Museum [53] alludes to Stephen Covey and comes up with 6 Habits of Highly Empathic People:

- Cultivate curiosity about strangers. To cultivate empathy in this way requires a curiosity that is keen to understand the world from the other person's viewpoint. It is more than idle chatter. A previous section has spoken about the role of curiosity in creativity. (see pp 38-40)   That section can just as easily be applied to empathy.
- Challenge prejudices and discover commonalities. It is all too easy to have prejudices about other people (gender, age, religion, ethnicity, social class etc.) By challenging our own and others prejudices, we begin to break down the barriers of difference and become more empathic towards other people. Doing so we begin to discover our shared and common humanity.
- Listen hard – and open up. Listening is covered elsewhere in this book. (see pp 95-98)
- Inspire mass action and social change. Roman Krznaric is keenly aware of the link between empathy and social change, having written articles for Oxfam, the UN Development Program, and Friends of the Earth. He has written also about the role of empathy in combating climate change. Because of this, he is an advocate of teaching empathy in schools and attempting to discover how social networking can harness empathy for mass social action. Krznaric notes that empathy can transform our underlying thinking patterns, as well as shifting our priorities from extrinsic values to intrinsic ones.[54]
- Develop an ambitious imagination. In case the above suggests that empathy is primarily directed towards those on the margins

---

[53] The Empathy Museum launched in 2015 in London. It is an experiential arts space and intends touring internationally. www.empathymuseum.com

[54] Krznaric, Roman. March 2015.

of society, then Krznaric says "no." We have the capacity to empathise with anyone (as noted earlier, including others' happiness). Importantly, notes Krznaric, we need to empathise with those we do not agree with, and who we might otherwise think of as "enemies." The imagination Krznaric refers to here is that of shifting our attention from the 20th century "Age of Introspection" to gazing outward and seeing the possibilities that arise when we become interested in the lives of others – the "Age of Empathy."

- Try another person's life. This method puts into practice the "walk a mile in another's moccasins" proverb. (See box). Sometimes we can do this just by thinking about it, but the real test is to actually experience someone else's life. We may not all be able to do what George Orwell did and spend time tramping the streets of London or living on the breadline in Paris, which gave him the material for his first full-length work, *Down and Out in Paris and London*. However, we may be able to spend a night at a homeless refuge or help out in a soup kitchen to get some inkling of another's life.

> **Walking a Mile**
> The proverb to walk a mile in another's moccasins has been attributed to various Native American tribes, but it appears that the phrase originated in a 1895 poem by Mary T Lathrap, titled *Judge Softly*, the first stanza of which is:
> *Pray, don't find fault with the man that limps,*
> *Or stumbles along the road.*
> *Unless you have worn the moccasins he wears,*
> *Or stumbled beneath the same load.*

We may not have to do as George Orwell did. It appears that by simply reading *Down and Out in Paris and London* and similar books, we can develop and increase our empathy. But not just any sort of book will work.

In 2013 researchers divided participants in a study into four groups.[55] The four groups were given four different reading tasks. One group read non-fictional work, a second group read genre (or popular) fiction, a third read literary fiction, and the fourth group read nothing. Following their reading, each of the participants took a test that measured their ability to infer and understand other people's thoughts and emotions.

The results following the reading of nonfiction or popular fiction ranged from unimpressive to insignificant. Those who read literary fiction, however, consistently scored higher. What's the difference between popular and literary fiction? This is within the realm of literary criticism which is outside the scope of this book. However, a brief explanation of the difference is needed in order to make sense of this research.

Popular fiction tends to be exciting and has a wide range of (mostly unexplored) emotional responses. Within popular fiction the characters are often stereotyped and their responses tend to be consistent and predictable. Literary fiction, on the other hand, often gets "into the head" of its characters, with the reader having to imagine more and discover for themselves the psychology of the characters and the relationships they have. The reader of literary fiction has to take on the minds of the novel's characters. The reader is almost compelled to empathise.

The reader of literary fiction is taken on new, often unexpected, journeys of the mind. Literary fiction disrupts, undermines, and challenges the reader's ideas, prejudices and notions of other people. It helps the reader to understand people who are different in some way.

Another study, in 2014,[56] discovered that when we read about the experience a character is having in a novel then the part of the

---

[55] Kidd, David Comer & Castano, Emanuele. 2013
[56] Wehbe, Murphy, Talukdar, Fyshe, Ramdas, and Mitchell, PLoS One. 2014; 9(11)

brain that is lit up is the same part of the brain that lights up when we are having that same experience. So, by reading about an experience, our mind perceives it very much as if we are living that experience ourselves.

Roman Krznaric is a fan of George Orwell and his novel, *Down and Out in Paris and London*. Krznaric describes how he links empathy and social change in the novels of Orwell. *"The traditional way to think about social change is about changing political institutions – new laws, new policies, overthrowing governments and so on. I think social change is actually about creating a revolution of human relationships. About changing the way people treat each other on an everyday basis. That's what Orwell was learning about. He was talking to individuals – understanding the minutiae of their lives – and after his time living in the streets of London he went on to do journalistic work which was really about trying to connect with human lives."*

It may be tempting to think that it is possible to forego reading a novel and watch the movie instead and still gain the benefit of enhanced empathy. Be warned – it may not be so. Certainly, some movies can evoke an empathic response; think of the lyrics from the 1961 song: *sad movies always make me cry*. The advantage of novels, however, is that the internal dialogue of characters is embedded within the novel. Internal dialogue is often missing or gets lost in a movie. The attention of the viewer is distracted by special effects, big-name actors, or the scene setting.

That other favourite alternative to reading – television watching – fares even worse than movies when it comes to enhancing empathy: its effect can actually be negative. Research involving pre-schoolers in 2013 found that pre-schoolers who are exposed to more TV than others have a "weaker understanding of other people's beliefs and desires, and reduced cognitive development."[57]

---

[57] Quoted in *www.psychologytoday.com/blog/the-athletes-way/201412/can-reading-fictional-story-make-you-more-empathetic*, accessed 24 May 2016

Before leaving the discussion on empathy it is worth noting that although we often associate empathy with becoming aware of, or understanding, the feelings and thoughts of others, we can also empathise with the actions and bodily movements of others. Noticing another person's bodily actions, stance, and/or gestures, can help us empathise with them. When listening to someone else, often the mirroring of that person's posture can help us listen more creatively. Creative listening leads to greater empathy. (See box pp 94-98)

Trust

Is trust a precursor to encouragement, or is it that behaving in an encouraging manner is likely to help build trust? Like most human interactions it is a bit of both, neither one nor the other, but rather that the two are interconnected in much the same way as asking which came first: the chicken or the egg? It can be claimed with some validity though that the building of trust is crucial to enabling people to be open, transparent, giving, collaborative and creative in any one-on-one or group setting.

Research on trust in marriage for example, often shows that trust is more important than love as a predictor of whether a couple will remain together. In the business setting it is now widely accepted that the greater the level of trust within a company, the greater the productivity and morale and the less the turnover of staff.

Those who study social capital also note the crucial part that trust plays in helping to provide the "social glue" that binds a community together. It is no surprise to find that communities with low social capital and low levels of trust have greater levels of crime, less philanthropy, lower academic achievement and even greater health problems. The father of "Social Capital," Robert Putnam, wrote about the decline of trust in the United States.[58] When asked "how do you change all this?" Putnam allegedly replied, "I don't really know." Perhaps this book can be one that helps to provide a glimpse of how the slide into distrust can be averted.

---

[58] Putnam, Robert. 2000

So, what helps to build trust? A couple of the elements of trust building will be explored in more depth below. Amongst the immensity of literature on the subject these four factors emerge as predominant:

- Listening. (See below).
- Honesty. Honesty implies being open not only to one's thoughts but also to one's feelings and communicating those in a transparent, compassionate, manner. It means taking responsibility (response-ability) for one's mistakes and not attempting to blame another. Being honest also means acknowledging one's limitations or lack of knowledge. If I do not know something I will not pretend otherwise.
- Reliability. If I say that I will do something, then I will do it. If I am unable to complete what I have said I will do then I will be honest and admit I am unable to do so.
- Encouraging. By being encouraging one builds trust and as trust builds one becomes encouraged.

Listening

Much has been written about the art of listening over the past half century, with various descriptive labels: *creative listening* and *active listening* being two of the most common. The reason that all these add an adverb before the word listening is to distinguish the method from that of passive hearing that most of us meet on a day-to-day basis. Passive hearing is not fully attentive, it is a hearing in which we may hear the words but not really appreciate their meaning or their significance to the speaker.

Creative/active listening, on the other hand, is a process that fully engages with the speaker so that the speaker is fully heard, fully understood, and fully acknowledged. (See the box for a brief description of some of the techniques of creative listening). I shall use simply the term "creative listening" in keeping with the first word of the **COFFEE** acronym.

Creative listening is a skill that can be learnt much like any other skill. Growing up, we may assume that we learn how to listen, but often all we have learnt is a passive hearing of the message of another person. Much of what passes for conversation can simply be one person waiting for a gap in what the other person is saying for them to step into and have their say. An analogy that helps to illustrate this habit is to visualise the speaker holding onto a helium filled balloon. In that balloon is the story that they are speaking about. When the listener intrudes and butts in with their own story it is as if they have stolen the balloon from the first speaker and now hold onto that balloon as if it is their own. How often do you notice people "stealing other people's balloons"? Often enough, I would guess, that we can wonder how it is that people ever get to finish their story, or at least have it told in such a way that the listener has fully understood it.

Creative listening is so much more; it is a process that the listener actively engages in, with the intent of fully and truly understanding and appreciating what the speaker is saying.

Besides the techniques in the box (see p 100), creative listening means being fully present in the conversation, not being distracted by the time, passers-by or the beautiful pattern of the wallpaper behind the speaker. Creatively listening also means suspending judgments, letting go of one's opinions and allowing oneself to fully understand what the other person is saying. This does not mean that the listener must agree with the speaker. It does, however, mean putting aside disagreement long enough to enable the listener to fully understand what the speaker is saying.

Indeed, before responding with one's own opinion it is worthwhile for the listener to summarise what they have understood the speaker to be saying so that the speaker knows that they have been understood. Summarising in this way means that the listener has truly understood and has not just waited until such time that they can talk about their opinions or thoughts.

Often we can be uncomfortable with silence, yet silence can be a powerful element in a creative listening conversation. Some people like to organise their thoughts in their mind before they verbalise them, whereas others think their thoughts out loud - by

---

Some Creative Listening Techniques

Mirroring: Taking a pose that is similar to that of the speaker. For example, if the speaker has their hands on the table in front of them, then the listener would also lay their hands on the table.

Reflecting: A speaker may use a word or a phrase at the end of a thought. Reflecting that word or phrase back encourages the speaker to continue or to expand on the thought. Reflecting also helps the speaker to realise that they have been accurately listened to.

Paraphrasing: Closely related to reflecting, paraphrasing is summarising in the listeners words what it is that they have understood the speaker to have said. This enables the speaker to know that they have been accurately heard and to correct any misapprehension that the listener may have.

Non-verbal Actions: It is important to realise that communication involves so much more than the words being spoken (or heard). For the listener this means using non-verbal actions that show an interest in what the speaker is saying. A simple smile, a nod of the head or eye contact help to convey such attention. A word of caution however; in some cultures eye contact can be interpreted as a sign of rudeness, so be warned.

Clarification: Questions of a clarifying nature can be useful to help a speaker know that they have been listened to and to more fully explore what it is they wish to convey.

Positive Reinforcement: Words such as "go on," "tell me more," can be encouraging but should be used sparingly so as not to become distracting. Words that imply agreement (e.g. "yes," "very good," or "indeed") can become annoying and it is usually better to wait until a time when it is appropriate to indicate why the listener is in agreement.

---

speaking. The former is characteristic of those with introversion tendencies. It is important to recognise this in communication and not think that just because there is a space – a silence – we must jump in with our tongues and fill it up. As the old 60s song goes: silence is golden.

When did you last listen to silence? If you haven't made a conscious effort to find silence in your life, then I would hazard to guess that it is quite some time since you entered a space of silence. No matter where we attune our ears in today's society, there will usually be noise, chatter, clatter, the roar of traffic, music blaring, or some audio-intrusion. Indeed, most of the places that we come together for social interaction are noisy: our office spaces, cafés and bars, shopping centres, not even the hallowed halls of libraries today seem to be immune.

A lot of the human race is quite comfortable with or at least accepting of, noise. But those on the introversion end of the introversion-extroversion spectrum are less so. When it comes to being encouraging, we need to also be aware of encouraging those on the introversion end of the continuum. (See pp 105-106).

Before moving on to the next section, a quick word on the techniques of creative listening. When first being exposed to these techniques and learning them, the process and interactions with people can feel clinical, as if they were devoid of human warmth and emotion. My advice would be threefold. First – persevere, the rewards are worth it. Second – if you can, find someone else with whom to practice these techniques, perhaps even a creative listening course where there are others who are willing to give it a try. Third – most learning goes through a four-step process, as shown in the diagram below.

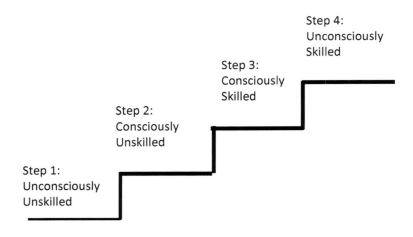

Step 4:
Unconsciously
Skilled

Step 3:
Consciously
Skilled

Step 2:
Consciously
Unskilled

Step 1:
Unconsciously
Unskilled

Before we begin any skills development journey, we may not even know that we don't know the skill. We are Unconsciously Unskilled. Then we take the next step and discover that we do not know the skill or that we are less skilled at it than we thought we were. We are now Consciously Unskilled. We decide to do something about our unskilled state and we start to learn new skills or add to those we already know. We are now becoming Consciously Skilled. Once we have fully mastered the skills and immersed ourselves in them, we find that we are Unconsciously Skilled. We now use the skills as if they had always been part of our make-up.

Think of learning to ride a bicycle. Before getting on we watch others riding along and may think to ourselves "that looks easy, I can do that." Then we get on a bicycle for the first time and immediately fall off. "Maybe," we say to ourselves, "this isn't as easy as it looks." We realise that we do not have the bicycle-riding skills. But we persevere, we ask someone to help us, maybe an adult teaches us. After a while, we are riding around the backyard, but all the while having to think, "hands on handlebars, stay balanced, keep pedalling." We are cycling, but we are very conscious of doing so. Eventually, we just get on our bicycle and pedal off, not having to think about it anymore – we are Unconsciously Bicycle-Skilled.

However, in steps 2 and 3 the skills and techniques we are learning can sound and feel clinical and mechanistic. In a sense they are, that is because we are thinking about them, we are practising certain aspects and getting feedback on how we are doing.

Eventually, however, we are able to incorporate creative listening skills into our everyday, normal conversation, without thinking about them. The techniques become part of our listening and communicating style. Once we have done that we will find that the way in which we use the techniques become our own.

Speaking and Talking

Listening is an important encouraging skill to bring to conversations. However, conversations involve speaking also, and the ways in which we speak should also be encouraging. There is an acronym that has become popular recently with it appearing in many forms on Facebook, Twitter, Instagram and elsewhere. The exact source of the acronym is not known although a poem published in 1872 by Mary Ann Pietzker may be one of its antecedents. The poem's title is *Is It True? Is It Necessary? Is It Kind?* The acronym itself reminds us that before we speak we should **THINK** and ask ourselves:

- Is it **T**rue?
- Is it **H**onest?
- Is it **I**nspiring?
- Is it **N**ecessary?
- Is it **K**ind?

Kinda cute huh? (You may have discovered by now that I am a fan of acronyms). Cute or not, the acronym is very useful, because it does capture the elements that make our speech encouraging, as well as being a useful mnemonic to bring to mind during our conversations.

We should also be mindful of timing. Even though what we want to say may comply with all the ingredients of THINK, it may not be the right time for it to be said. The author Kay Lindahl[59] recommends that we shift our thinking and speech from "What do I want to say?" to "What wants to be said?" She notes that the former is driven by our ego, whereas the latter is more associated with the spirit within which the conversation is being held. Our ego incites us to say something in order to make ourselves seem knowledgeable. When we converse within the spirit what we say arises from a need to be said within the conversation. It aids the co-creation of conversation that is mutually beneficial and expands the understanding, awareness, and consciousness of all involved, including the speaker.

But what about freedom of speech? Of course, we must uphold our right to freedom of speech, but we do not need to do so by neglecting respectful speech. When the offices of the French magazine Charlie Hebdo were bombed in January 2015 much of Europe responded with *Je Suis Charlie* placards proclaiming the right to free speech. However, once free speech descends into racial abuse, religious intolerance, or the violent speech of domestic violence, then that freedom has been abused. It is possible to have an honest conversation, where differing views are stated, without that conversation becoming abusive, intolerant, or disrespectful. It does mean that we must THINK first though.

The range of speech patterns that contribute towards non-encouraging encounters are many. A few that we should be aware of include: insults, name calling, sarcasm, finding fault, threats, dominating the conversation, continually correcting, humiliation, lying, and yelling or shouting.

Being Present

Have you ever been talking with someone and whilst you are saying something you notice their eyes wander around the room, or

---

[59] Lindahl, Kay. 2003.

they pick up their coffee cup and play with it? Off-putting isn't it? You realise that they are not paying attention. They are not present.

Yet, being present is vital if we are going to be encouraging listeners. It has been estimated that we can speak about 125 words per minute, but that our mind can think at about 400 words per minute. So, there is a lot of wiggle room there for our mind to wander and to find something else to "listen" to. You would think that this would not be a problem because obviously, you have plenty of capacity to listen to what the speaker says and pay attention to something else at the same time. Wrong!

Studies show that immediately after a short spoken presentation those who were apparently listening could recall only 50% of what was said. Within 48 hours that level of comprehension drops to just 25%. Even though we apparently have the capacity to pay attention to more than one thing, our comprehension, when we are not present, suffers significantly.

Communication, particularly face-to-face communication, is so much more than the words that are spoken and listened to. Tone of voice, posture, eye contact, facial expressions, gestures – all these and more contribute to the communication. Collectively they are known as non-verbal communication. You may have read or heard that just 7% of communication is the actual words used and the other 93% is non-verbal. However, these figures have been largely discredited as being of little use in the field of communication studies. The key point is to recognise that in face-to-face communication, the non-verbal contributions are just as important as the verbal contributions.[60] This is how we can use the "spare capacity" of thinking speed versus speaking speed. We can use it to pay attention to the speaker's non-verbal communication. Is their non-verbal communication in accord with what they are saying, or is it telling us something different?

---

[60] Non-verbal communication though, can be culture-specific. A gesture (e.g. the thumbs up signal) can mean approval in one culture, but is offensive in another. The topic of cross-cultural communication is not something that is addressed in this book. The reader is encouraged to seek out other resources, especially if their encounters are between cultures.

Does the non-verbal communication add extra information or "flavour" to the words? Perhaps the most useful way of using this "spare capacity" is to continually ask ourselves whether we are paying attention to the speaker. Am I being present? If we find we are not, we can use this spare capacity to bring ourselves back to the present, back to being attentive and encouraging.

Being present is also about us as the listener. When we are present we notice our own reactions and feelings. What is happening in our body? Are we becoming tense? Are we feeling comfortable? When we are present it is much easier to notice that we get distracted. We become aware of other thoughts much quicker. When we do notice that a distracting thought has arisen, we can simply acknowledge it, perhaps name it ("oh, there's an extraneous thought"), and simply let it go and return our attention to the speaker. No need to push it away, just let it go. When we do this, our presence is noticed (perhaps not consciously) by the speaker and they feel encouraged.

Suspending Judgment

You are part way through telling someone about an idea you've had. The person you are telling this to interrupts you saying, "No, that's not correct. You're wrong." You've been judged, and it's not a nice feeling, is it? What happens next depends on a number of things; the relationship you already have, how you are feeling at the time, the location, your (and their) understanding of conflict resolution. Whatever, it is unlikely that you feel encouraged. Plus, instead of exploring your idea you and the listener are probably now engaged in an argument about an idea that you haven't even had a chance to fully outline.

In order to creatively listen to someone, we must suspend judgment. Notice that I am not saying that you must agree with the other person. Rather it is about suspending making judgments sufficiently to enable the speaker to fully explain their thoughts. Crucially too, judgment needs to be suspended in order for you (the listener) to fully understand what the speaker is saying.

Coming as it does from the legal system judgment has a sense of finality about it. There is a sense that once something has been judged then that is the end of the story, no more arguments will be listened to. There is no right of appeal. This is quite contrary to being an encouraging listener. An encouraging listener is keen to open up dialogue, to broaden the scope, to explore all possibilities. A judgmental listener will tend to shut down the conversation, closing off any avenues towards exploration and understanding.

Nonviolent Communication

For a young man with a Jewish name, growing up in Detroit during the 1940s and 1950s, it was always going to be rough. So it was for Marshall Rosenberg. What the young Rosenberg felt hurt by was not so much the beatings he received but the smiles of the onlookers. These experiences led him to ponder the roots of violence and how we could relate to one another in a non-violent way, yet respecting our differences. Marshall Rosenberg decided to study Clinical Psychology at the University of Wisconsin to help him in his quest. There he studied under Carl Rogers,[61] and it is from him that Rosenberg learnt the value of empathic listening and integrating our thoughts, feelings, values and words. He graduated with a Ph.D. from there in 1961 and then went on to work with Civil Rights campaigners often helping to mediate between rioting students and college administrators.

All of this study and experience resulted in Marshall Rosenberg developing Nonviolent Communication (NVC). NVC is now a well-established theoretical and practical communication technique that has been taught in more than 60 countries.

At the core of NVC are four interlocking practices:

- Observation: We simply see, taste, and hear what is happening around us.

---

[61] Carl Rogers (1902-1987) was one of the founders of a humanist approach to psychology and developed the person-centred approach. He is also credited with coining the term "encounter group" although the basic idea of encounter groups had developed earlier.

- Feelings: From our observations, we will notice that we feel something and become attuned to that without attempting to judge, criticise, or evaluate. Being able to do so means that we differentiate between feeling and thinking.
- Needs/Values: We all have needs and/or values that contribute to our sense of well-being. NVC suggests that when our needs are met we experience "good" feelings. When our needs are not met we experience "bad" feelings. The knack is to be able to recognise what our needs and values are so that we are not tossed and turned by unruly emotions and feelings.
- Requests: Once we have observed something, become attuned to the feelings that arise inside us, and recognise what need or value that feeling is pointing to; we are in a better position to be able to make our requests. We are able to request of others instead of demanding or exploiting them.

As the word itself suggests, communication is a two-way (or multi-way) process. Communication stems from the same root as *common*, in other words, what is shared by all, what is public. Because it is a two-way process NVC recognises that the four practices briefly outlined above are expressed via the way we give and receive them. We give honestly and receive empathically.

This very brief overview is not intended to be a complete or even partial exploration of the depth of NVC. It is intended to make the reader aware (if not already so) of NVC as a practice that, when used, will aid in encouraging others in our encounters.

Encouraging Introversion

Anywhere from a third to half the human race is inclined towards the introversion end of the introversion-extroversion continuum. Those on this end of the spectrum process stimuli in a quite different way from those on the other end of the spectrum. Whereas an extrovert will process information and respond to it by speaking and seeking the voices of others, an introvert is more inclined to find themselves most inspired or creative when there is opportunity for quiet reflection.

A person on the introversion end of the spectrum is more at home reflecting upon information internally, sorting out their own thoughts and feelings within, before speaking. This is the opposite of those from the spectrum's other end, who tend to work out their thoughts by speaking them.

In group settings it is not surprising, then, to find the discussion dominated by those from the extrovert end of the spectrum. This is not a criticism of extroverted people; rather it is a recognition that groups are more inclined to listen to and be led by, those who appear more charismatic, outgoing and sure of their thoughts and ideas. But charisma and fine-sounding oratory is no guarantee of wisdom. Regrettably, our culture has advanced the "extrovert ideal"[62] over the introverted approach so that extroverts will gain attention, and their ideas given greater credence, more often than those of introverts.

Hence, if at least a third of people are likely to be on the introversion side of the introvert-extrovert spectrum, then in order to encourage them to participate and offer their opinions, thoughts and ideas, it is important to find ways of allowing for quiet time, a silent space to be present in our conversations and dialogues.

Before moving on from this brief discussion, it is important to note that people on the introverted end of the spectrum often find crowds distressing and are likely to withdraw. Yet, put them up on a stage, in front of a crowd of people, and a person with introversion tendencies will come to life. It's as if they are able to mentally withdraw from the crowd and enter their own highly creative space and now have a stage on which to express it. Just don't expect them to enter the small-talk later with the same degree of expressiveness.

---

[62] The "Extrovert Ideal" is a term coined by Susan Cain in her book *Quiet: The Power of Introverts in a World That Can't Stop Talking*. The extrovert ideal, according to Cain, has come to be the omnipresent ideal of self-hood in modern western-styled cultures.

Questions Again

In the chapter on **Creativity,** there was a sub-section entitled *Question, Question, Question.* The work of Warren Berger was introduced to show that creativity had a lot more to do with the questions that were asked than with the answers that were obtained. The same is true for encouragement. Using a compassionate questioning technique can be highly encouraging for many people.

In most cases, an open question is more likely to be encouraging than is a closed question. An open question is one that allows the person being questioned to open up further, to explore more and to tell their story more fully. A closed question, however, is more likely to lead to a very short, closed off conversation, as the answer will often be a simple "yes," "no," or a very short phrase that provides the questioner with very little feedback. Here are some simple examples of open and closed questions:

Open Questions	Closed Questions
What inspires you?	Do you feel anxious?
How do you deal with that situation?	This is the best way to do it – isn't it?
Why is this important to you?	Are you happy?
What happened next?	Did you speak to the manager?
Tell me more about that?	That's true, don't you think?

Notice that the examples of closed questions are likely to be answered with a simple "yes" or "no," whereas the open questions are likely to indicate to the person being questioned that you have a genuine interest in their full answer. Notice too, that open questions are more likely to be neutral in tone, whereas a closed question can suggest judgment or a sense of superiority. Open questions are far more encouraging.

In the examples above, one of the open questions begins with "why." Beginning a question with *why?* can sometimes sound invasive or overly critical. Warren Berger suggests softening such questions by beginning, for example, with something like: "I'm curious, why is it …?" or "I'd be interested to know why…?"

Humour

Most of us enjoy a good laugh. We also enjoy the company of people who make us laugh and/or those that laugh along with us. Humour can do much to encourage those whom we encounter. Having a sense of humour is one of the human aspects that most people say they look for when deciding on friendships and especially on partnerships.

Encouraging humour however is not just the ability to remember and relate a series of jokes. Jokes that are racist, sexist, or in other ways aggressive, do not encourage. Indeed, such humour (if it can be called that) will tend to discourage. Charlie Chaplin (perhaps one of the greatest comedians to have ever lived) put it very well when he noted that: *"My pain may be the reason for somebody's laugh. But my laugh must never be the reason for somebody's pain."*

The type of humour that Chaplin was at pains to be wary of includes ridicule, put-down type jokes, sarcasm, overdone teasing (which can deteriorate into a perception of bullying). Such humour ignores the feelings that may be induced in the listener (whether they be the direct butt of the joke or not) and hence do not qualify here as encouraging type humour.

Encouraging type humour has been given a name by researchers[63] – affiliative humour. Affiliative humour is the type of humour that seeks to put people at ease, decrease tension, or help establish relationships. It is humour that, whilst being funny, does no harm to either party. Not only does this type of humour encourage

---

[63] Yes, there are people who study humour: there is even an *International Society for Humor Studies* (www.humorstudies.org) which puts out a quarterly journal and holds an annual international conference.

others, it is also good for individual well-being. It is associated with increased self-esteem, emotional stability, openness and decreased levels of depression and anxiety.

Food, Glorious Food

Talking involves the use of our mouth. So does eating. Food can be one of the best ways of encouraging conversations and dialogue. When I was growing up, the dining table was the focus for many conversations, it was where I learnt to converse. Sadly, the dinner time conversations in many families have dwindled over the past few decades. Food remains, however, a great catalyst for encouraging encounters.

In Māori society (the indigenous people of New Zealand) formal dialogue cannot take place until food and drink have been shared. Visitors are welcomed by a process called powhiri, including greetings and an outline of the purpose of the hui (meeting). Visitors and hosts then repair to the dining hall to share food. Once food has been shared then, and only then, can the purpose of meeting together be fully discussed. It is a time-honoured tradition that enables visitors and hosts to come together, discover each other, and so enter the dialogue as a combined group (rather than two separate groups).

Many years ago a colleague of mine shared the following story with me. Michael was working as a Community Development Advisor on the eastern side of Christchurch. One evening he attended a meeting called by the Department of Housing to discuss housing issues for local residents – an enormous problem at the time. Many people in the area were homeless, living in crowded accommodation or finding it difficult to pay the rents in the area. The meeting was held in a community hall with chairs arranged in rows and a table at the front, behind which the Department's officials sat. Off to the side of the main hall was a kitchen, and in it a number of local women were baking, cooking and making tea for refreshments for those in the hall.

Michael told me how he sat in the hall listening to the government representatives and the questions that local residents (mostly men) were putting to them. Whether he got bored, or curious I cannot recall, but at some stage he left the hall and went into the kitchen. There he found the women busily preparing food and drink – and discussing the issues that were being debated in the hall. Michael stopped to listen. He became captivated, because there, in the kitchen, away from the formal setting, the conversation was far closer to the lived reality of people in the area. The women that Michael listened to had a much clearer understanding of the issues in the area and some of the possible solutions.

As Michael recounted this story I got an image of a large family kitchen table, with people sitting around it, a cup of tea in front of them, maybe flour covering their wrists. The image was of jovial informality, yet with the discussion involving a deep understanding of local reality.

This book has put forward the **COFFEE** acronym as a way of thinking about a way of working. But it is also suggests that sitting down over a cup of coffee (or tea, or a muffin, or a full 3-course meal) is a simple and encouraging way of encountering one another.

Don't forget food – the heart of hospitality, and encouragement.

Time

Question: How much time does it take to be encouraging? Answer: As long as it takes.

Our western approach to time has been immersed in the same linear approach as has much of the rest of our lives. When it comes to problem-solving, decision-making, or simply exploring an issue, we often constrain ourselves within a definite, and pre-determined time-frame. Activist groups come together for a meeting with a built-in expectation that the meeting will last one hour, two hours, a day, or however long we have allocated to it.

Many indigenous cultures, however, treat time in a different manner. For many, the meeting takes as long as it needs to for the group to arrive at a point where there is nothing more that needs to be said, acknowledged, or decided. In the section on listening, I introduced the Aboriginal concept of dadirri. (See p 41) Dadirri speaks also of the use of time in this way: *"We don't like to hurry. There is nothing more important than what we are attending to. There is nothing more urgent that we must hurry away for."*

If we think about this for a moment, we can understand how being pressured by our concept of time can be discouraging rather than encouraging. If we enter into an encounter with others without a time limit, without a sense of having to be somewhere else, then not only does that project an attitude of encouragement, it also means that we are less likely to skip over or miss creative opportunities.

We noticed in the section on **Flow** that when we are in the state of flow time becomes meaningless. When we are "in flow" then hours can go by without us noticing. Being concerned about time disrupts this sense of flow.

Giving people the "time of day" is a highly encouraging thing to do. Giving people your time says "I care."

XI
ENCOUNTERS

Human Beings have survived on this planet for the past 200,000 years or more because of our tendency to cooperate, to work together, to be altruistic – in short because we encountered one another in encouraging ways.

There is a misconception, in western society at least, that we have survived through competition. Competition with beast and other animals, competition with nature, competition with each other. But this misconception is due in large part to a misunderstanding and misreading of Charles Darwin, the father of evolution. Although most of the population have not read either of his famous works, *Origin of Species* and *The Descent of Man*, most of us will equate Darwin with the phrase "survival of the fittest."[64] The "fittest" in this phrase has come to be synonymous with meaning that those who rise to the top of the pile in a struggle of competition and dominance are those who will survive and inherit their "rightful" place as leaders, the richest, or the most powerful.

Darwin, however, used the term "fit" in quite a different sense. As a biologist, Darwin understood the connections between species and had begun to recognise the relatedness of eco-systems. As such, Darwin understood "fit" to mean that those species best able to adapt and fit into the available niches within an eco-system were more likely to survive. The sense with which Darwin used the term was much like finding the right "fit" for a jigsaw piece. The piece fits exactly and does so because of the accommodating relationship it has with its neighbouring pieces. In fact, Darwin was so incensed that his

---

[64] In fact, the phrase "survival of the fittest" does not come from Darwin at all. It was coined by Herbert Spencer, an English philosopher and contemporary of Darwin's.

theory had been used to proclaim "might is right" that he grumbled about it in a letter to his friend, the geologist Charles Lyell.[65]

Thus, notwithstanding the misrepresentation of Darwin and the many apologists for competition, dominance, and oppression that have existed since, we are still able to enter into encounters that are mutually beneficial, creative and rewarding.

Having said that, it may be surprising that the word "encounter" is used here. If you look up the word "encounter" in any dictionary you will find that the first definition will be similar to this one: "meet as adversary." However, the second meaning – "meet by chance or unexpectedly" – is the sense in which it is used here. Within the context of this book and acronym, the meaning has been further broadened to include meetings that are deliberately arranged.

Chance Encounters

How often do we hear people say that "it was just a chance encounter?" Often when someone says that, they then go on to talk about the "encounter" having been memorable, important or useful to them in some way. Meeting someone unexpectedly or by chance always entails the possibility of something emerging from the encounter that neither partner was previously aware of or even thinking about. Activators need to be aware of this possibility and eagerly seek the opportunities that arise from such encounters.

Encounters can occur at any time, in any place. A chance encounter on a bus or a brief chat with your local barista may provide just the spark needed to inspire a "creative opportunity." Being open to these encounters means that we must put aside any sense of higher knowledge, greater skills or superior wisdom. All human beings have knowledge and skills unique to them, that no-one else has. If we act in ways that suggest otherwise, then we both deny the other person

---

[65] *"I have received in a Manchester Newspaper a rather good squib, showing that I have proved 'might is right' & therefore that Napoleon is right & every cheating Tradesman is also right."* Letter by Charles Darwin to Charles Lyell, 1860. Quoted in Stefan Klein.

their uniqueness, identity and self-worth, and we discount the possibility that we may discover or learn something new.

The seemingly innocent or trivial encounter may contain within it the seeds of something much greater, akin to the Butterfly Effect introduced earlier in this book. If you stop to think about it, the Butterfly Effect of chance encounters can be seen in your own life. Take a moment to reflect on your life and think of some of the most memorable or important experiences in your life and how they came to be. Chances are that many of these will have involved some form of chance encounter. Be it meeting your future spouse, or perhaps being lent a life-changing book by a friend, or maybe simply someone telling you about the best deal on a used car.

The American psychologist, Albert Bandura, was one of the first psychologists to explore chance encounters. In a paper he wrote in 1982[66] he cites the case of a graduate student who was sick of reading an assignment and decided to go play golf with a buddy. In front of the two of them they saw two attractive woman golfers. As Bandura notes *"before long the two twosomes become one foursome and, in the course of events, one of the partners becomes the wife of the graduate golfer."* It is a typical story and one that many of us can relate to. For Bandura, it was especially poignant for, as he goes on to recount, *"the graduate student in this particular case happens to be myself."*

Bandura was interested in how chance encounters *"set off causal chains in the same way as prearranged (encounters) do."* In doing so he looked at encounters that had both positive and negative outcomes. He noted that once we have had a chance encounter, the effects upon us influence our lives in much the same way as do pre-arranged or planned events and meetings.

Bandura noted in his paper that the unpredictability of the influence that a chance encounter may have on someone means that not only is it unpredictable but that social engineering is less possible than some science fiction authors would suggest. He also

---

[66] Bandura, Albert. July 1982.

acknowledged that chance encounters can have positive, negative or neutral outcomes. In the context of this book, it is the positive outcomes that we are seeking – the Creative Opportunities.

Research since Bandura into positive psychology has shown that by imagining positive futures we are able to experience positive futures. This suggests that if we enter into encounters with an optimistic or helpful frame of mind then the encounter has a greater chance of producing positive outcomes – creative opportunities.

Deliberate Encounters

Bringing people and communities together to discuss issues and to solve problems is an oft employed procedure for activators seeking social change. People meet together deliberately, for a common purpose, albeit they may have differing ideas, knowledge, and/or skills.

Until the mid-1900s the common way for this to happen in the western tradition was to meet in an organised, often hierarchic manner, utilising *Robert's Rules of Order* (originally published in 1876). Sadly to say, today much of our official public decision-making bodies (parliaments, senates, city councils, boards, and committees) still opt for this style of meeting.

However, in the mid-1900s groups began experimenting with more creative styles of meeting. Recognising that process was as important as outcome, social change groups sought out ways to support the tasks of groups without neglecting the individual needs that each member brought to the group. Inspired by Quaker and other non-hierarchic traditions, these groups actively learnt about group dynamics, facilitation and consensus decision-making. Perhaps the seminal manual for social change groups at this time was the *Resource Manual for a Living Revolution*,[67] affectionately known as the *Monster Manual*. This manual, published in 1977, contained a wealth of techniques, exercises, and resources aiming to equip activators with

---

[67] Coover, Deacon, Esser & Moore. 1977.

the skills of non-hierarchic, non-violent, group decision-making processes and campaign techniques.

Since then the number of techniques for bringing people together to deliberate has mushroomed and expanded into many areas of social life. There are now innumerable societies and professional groupings dedicated to promoting these techniques and enhancing the skills of facilitators.[68] I shall not attempt to explain all of these techniques here, but will briefly summarise some of the more prevalent ones.

World Café

Imagine a café in which there are a dozen tables, with four or five seats at each. You and other participants arrive and seat yourselves at a table. On the table in front of you is some butcher paper, felt pens, crayons, maybe a "talking stick (or stone)" and perhaps even a vase of flowers. The café host introduces the concept, outlines the process, and sets the context of the conversations.

The café host poses a question relevant to the purpose of the meeting and for the next twenty minutes or so you and the three or four other café participants at your table discuss that question. Someone records on the butcher paper the thoughts and ideas that emerge from your discussion. After twenty minutes (or whatever the allotted time is), you all get up and move separately to other tables. It may be useful to leave one person behind at the table so that they can briefly explain to the next group what your group came up with.

At the next table, you will be seated with a new group of three or four others. If there is someone who has remained behind they will explain where the previous group got to. The café host may introduce a new question for you to discuss, or you may be encouraged to build on the work of the previous group to the initial question.

This process – of moving on to a different table after twenty or so minutes – is repeated as many times as is necessary.

---

[68] For example: International Association of Facilitators, International Association for Public Participation, International Association for Community Development.

Once you have completed as many rounds as necessary, café participants are invited to share with the entire group any insights, discoveries or ideas that have emerged from the discussions. Recording these in words and/or pictures and images is useful and can be added to the recordings that already exist at each table. Participants are invited to move around the tables reading the notes on the butcher paper at each table.

The process has a number of benefits over the more traditional meeting. With only four or five people per table there is a greater chance that those who may not normally participate get a chance to do so. By moving on to another table with different people and being asked to build on what the previous group came up with ensures that people do not get stuck in just one line of thought. Moving from table to table enables people to connect with others in the group and to use the diverse, collective wisdom of the group.

For further information you may wish to check out the following website: http://www.theworldcafe.com

Future Search

Future Search is a planning process that moves through five phases: the past, the present, the future, common ground, and action planning. Typically, each of these phases will take up a morning or afternoon session, meaning that the entire search can last 2 ½ to 3 days. The method is over thirty years old and has been used in a variety of settings worldwide, and has been found to work well with diverse groups.

A Future Search is predicated on four principles:

- Working with the whole system, by ensuring that a cross-section of all those involved are invited to participate.
- Laying out the "whole elephant" before attempting to solve any part of it. This ensures that everyone knows the full extent of what they are dealing with.
- Ensuring that the future and common ground are placed at the forefront of action plans, and that past conflict or problems are treated as information and not as something to be acted upon.

- Encouraging participants to take responsibility for actions not only after the Search but also during it.

The first phase of the process (the Past) is one in which a timeline related to the topic is constructed using the stories of individuals in the group.

Phase 2 (the present) is then constructed using a mind map of the trends that are impacting participants and their communities here and now. Group members can then identify the key issues/trends, and outline ways in which those key issues/trends are currently being dealt with. It is helpful here for those present to be open with those actions that they are proud of, as well as those they are not proud of (or are sorry for.)

In phase 3 participants put themselves in the future and describe what that looks, feels and acts like as if they were currently living it. Phase 4 (common grounds) are then identified by the diverse groups present. The dialogue around identifying common ground can take some time and should not be rushed.

The final phase (phase 5) is where action plans for getting to the desired future of common ground are discussed, agreed upon and participants sign up to.

For further information, you may wish to check out the following website: http://www.futuresearch.net/

Citizens' Juries (other similar techniques include: Community X-change, Citizens' Panels, Citizens' Councils, Consensus Conferences, or Citizen Assemblies)

The uniqueness of these methods is suggested in the name. We all know that juries are randomly selected from amongst the general citizenry, and that is the basis of Citizen's Juries. Many of the meetings (no matter how egalitarian, open and transparent we wish to make them) called by activators are mostly attended by those who self-select and usually have a vested interest in the matter under discussion at the meeting. A Citizens' Jury deliberately overturns this and participants are selected randomly. Because participants are selected randomly it is likely that a community (or society) will be represented more fairly, equally and equitably than are self-selection processes. Worldwide many local authorities and even national governments have used the Citizens' Jury approach to plan and/or advise the authority. The *Peoples Initiative* in Canada in 1991 mentioned on p 80 is an example of this type of encounter. Although it lends itself well to these environments and has been used as a mechanism for public consultation, there is no reason that NGOs or other activators should not use the process. Indeed, to counter the accusation of bias within these groups, this is a method that has untapped potential for these groups.

The concept was invented independently within the US and Germany[69] in the 1970s, although the inventor in each country did not discover the other until 1985. The US inventor, Ned Crosby, went on to set up the Jefferson Center which coined the term Citizens' Jury. Crosby's intention was to explore new democratic processes, of which the Citizens' Jury is the mainstay.

A traditional Citizens' Jury entails a randomly selected group of 15 – 24 people coming together for between three and five days. The "jurors" hear a range of expert opinion on whatever the issue at hand may be. Jurors may question the expert witnesses and then deliberate upon the best course of action from the perspective of the community they are representing. At the end of the process, the jurors make recommendations for policy makers and the public.

Further information can be found at:
http://jefferson-center.org/what-we-do/citizen-juries/
http://www.co-intelligence.org/CDCUsesAndPotency.html

Open Space (aka Unconference)

Those two words: Open and Space succinctly describe this technique. Often used for large workshops, symposia and conferences, Open Space begins with no set agenda. What could be more open than that? The technique provides a space, without

---

[69] Peter Dienel, in Germany designed planungszelle (Planning Cells) in the 1970s.

defining what should happen within that space. Thus, Open Space Technology as it is sometimes termed (I prefer Paul Born's term – Open Space Conversations[70]) is a true child of Complexity and Chaos Theories. It is organic, embraces diversity, is self- organising, and has no controlling group or body.

In the 1980s Harrison Owen noticed that when he went to conferences, some of the liveliest, most honest and creative conversations took place during the coffee breaks, the breaks between the formal sessions. He asked himself a simple question: Is it possible to combine the level of synergy and excitement present in a good coffee break, with the substantive activity and results characteristic of a good meeting?

Owen had also spent time during the 1960s in a West African village called Balamah and was enthralled to be part of a rite of passage process that lasted four days for the boys in the village. Owen says that at no time could he detect an organising or planning committee overseeing the proceedings, even though over 500 people participated. Owen's experience in Balamah was a long way from that of western approaches. What he did notice, however, was that the village was laid out in a circle, with an open space in the middle.

When Owen reflected on this experience and his question about the usefulness of coffee breaks, Open Space emerged. Owen experimented with his ideas and found that the concept worked if five pre-conditions existed:

1. There is an issue that people care about,
2. There is sufficient complexity that no-one person or small group can understand or solve the issue,
3. There is enough diversity amongst participants that there can be a great deal of skill, knowledge and expertise present,
4. There is passion present amongst the participants, even to the point that conflict may exist,
5. A sense of urgency exists.

---

[70] Born, Paul. 2008, 2012

Open Space Conversations involve five principles and one law. As you read through these you will notice how close to some of the ideas of emergence these principles come:

- Whoever comes are the right people.
- Whenever it starts is the right time to start.
- Wherever it is, is the right place.
- Whatever happens is the only thing that could have happened.
- When it's over – it's over.

And the one law is stated simply as The Law of Two Feet. This law places the responsibility for learning and contributing firmly in the hands of each participant. It says that if at any stage you feel bored, irritated or lose interest in whatever is going on in the space in which you are, then you can use your feet and move on.

So, how does it work? The ideal space includes a large open area in which all participants can sit in a circle, or concentric circles, and a series of four or more break-out spaces. With everyone seated in the large open space, the facilitator/convenor summarises the theme of the meeting and invites participants to spend a little time quietly thinking about and identifying issues or opportunities related to the theme. At the end of the time (say 10 minutes) the facilitator asks any participants who wish to come to the centre and announce their issue/opportunity and write a short (one sentence summary) on a sheet of paper and place it in a part of the space designated as the agenda area. Any person who does make such an announcement then takes responsibility for beginning that conversation, as well as reporting on it, with whoever turns up in one of the break-out areas.

Once all those who wish to have announced their topic, other participants write their name on the sheets of paper of the topics they are interested in. If there are more topics listed than there are break-out spaces available, it may be that topics are allocated a time frame (e.g. Session 1, Session 2 etc.) in which to hold those conversations.

Sounds too simple, doesn't it? Get people together who are passionate about a theme, allow them to identify the issues/opportunities, give them some space (and time), and don't

120

control the process or outcome. But it works. Self-organisation, spontaneity, diversity, and complexity can come together to create something wonderful.

If you wish to discover more, have a look at these websites:
http://openspaceworld.org/wp2/
http://www.mindviewinc.com/Conferences/OpenSpaces.html
(this includes a link to an 8-minute screencast about Open Space)

Appreciative Inquiry

Appreciative Inquiry diverges from the traditional problem-solving approach in that it begins with a search for the best in people, their culture, and the world. Rather than asking questions that attempt to discover the causes and roots of problems, Appreciative Inquiry asks questions that strengthen inherent potentials within people and their organisations. Quite simply it inquires into people and organisations in an appreciative manner. From that inquiry the process moves to visualising what might be, having conversations around what should be and finally, designing what will be. The four stages have been described as the four Ds: Discover, Dream, Design, Deploy.

The format can vary but one of the simplest is to get the group to split into pairs. Each pair then takes it in turn to be the interviewer and the interviewee. The interviewer asks questions designed to elicit from the interviewee the aspects of the topic that are (or were) successful, encouraging, supportive, educative etc. Use questions that focus on the story being told by the interviewee (e.g. "tell me more about that?" "how did that affect you?" "what did you contribute?") and that build on the strengths of the topic. The interviewer should make notes on what the strengths are, plus what contributes towards those strengths. Paul Born[71] uses the graphical analogy of a tree for the placement of these notes. The leaves of the tree represent the strengths, and the roots those things that contribute to the strengths.

---

[71] Born, ibid

Appreciative Inquiry moves conversations from questions that ask "what is wrong?" and "how can we fix it?" to "what do we have?" and "what are the opportunities here?" As such it is a technique that easily fits within the theme of this book.

For further information, check out these websites:

http://positivitystrategist.com/appreciative-inquiry-overview/

https://appreciativeinquiry.case.edu/intro/default.cfm

Charrette

In 19th century Paris architecture students worked feverishly on projects that had deadlines. At the end of that deadline, a charrette (from French, meaning *cart*) would come around, into which the students were to place their scale models and other work. Today it has come to refer to an "inquiry by design" process. Typically it is a process where a planning decision/design is required and there are social, environmental, economic and other complexities and a wide range of stakeholders.

A typical charrette may last several days or be spread over a number of weekends. Participants break into small groups to identify the issues and possible solutions involved. These deliberations are then collated and a draft plan designed. This is then presented back to the participants, who then break into small groups again to identify the issues and possible solutions that arise from that plan. This procedure is then iterated as many times as necessary.

The technique is one that is commonly used within urban planning and similar environments. As such the participants involved may not necessarily be highly representative of the community in which the plan is to be implemented.

Further information is available on these websites:

http://www.dse.vic.gov.au/effective-engagement/toolkit/tool-design-charrettes

http://www.charretteinstitute.org/charrette.html

PhotoVoice (aka Participatory photography)

We know that people use different learning modalities (auditory, visual, kinaesthetic/tactile, or a combination of all three). PhotoVoice is a method that purposely engages the visual modality. The principle is very simple: give people a camera (or get them to use the camera on their mobile phones) and ask them to take photographs of their community, so as to depict the community in all its reality. The technique is especially applicable for marginalised or forgotten communities. In a society in which the images that we are presented with are seen on TV, in the movies or in video games, the reality of life for those in marginalised communities is rarely seen. If it is seen at all, it is more than likely to be presented by someone from outside that community. This technique hands the medium for depiction to the community members themselves.

The process of photographing and depicting a community creates opportunities to make discoveries, form connections and can be a potent empowering activity.

For further information, you may wish to check out this website: https://photovoice.org/

The Inklings

During the 1930s and 1940s an unique group of writers, poets and literary enthusiasts formed at Oxford University. Calling themselves *The Inklings* (a deliberate play on the double meaning of the word), they had no formal agenda, no officers, and no rules. They met for the love of fantasy writing and the narrative style. They met to discuss their writing and ideas for plots or themes. Amongst them were two of the English-speaking world's notable fantasy novelists, C. S. Lewis and J. R. R. Tolkien. These two tried out some of their ideas that eventually became the literary masterworks *The Chronicles of Narnia, The Hobbit,* and *Lord of the Rings.*

One of the means by which this group developed ideas was that when a new idea came up within the group, each of the group members would write a chapter relating to that idea and then read it to the group.

The group drifted apart in 1949. Since then various literary groups around the world have named themselves after this group and are set up with similar objectives.

The method of writing a chapter relating to a new idea has occasionally been used within the social change movement, although there does not appear to be any social change technique named specifically after *The Inklings*. The method is worth exploring further as it incorporates both an individual and a group approach to ideas generation and development.

Facilitation

Facilitation has been a bit of a buzzword since the late 1960s and early 1970s. First picked up within the learning/encounter groups of that era and then by social change movements (particularly within non-violent action circles). Community development workers quickly picked up the ideas and it even attained a place within corporate circles late last century (albeit often used in a manner inconsistent with the original concept).

Many of the values, principles, and methods of facilitation have been with us for many years and held in traditional societies for centuries. The basic idea of facilitation is inherent in the very word itself. Facilitation derives from the French word *faciliter,* meaning *to render easy.* The idea of *making easy* is in contrast to the notion of chairing and Robert's Rules of Order which suggest a rigidness and procedural ways of doing things.

In order to make things easy - to facilitate - what does a facilitator need to remember? After almost forty years of learning about and applying the craft of facilitation, I have narrowed it down to just five concepts.

1. It's Not About Me. The facilitator is there to make it easy for a group to form their agenda, converse about that agenda and to make consensual decisions. The focus is not on the facilitator, it is on the maintenance of group processes and the task at hand. Lao Tzu said it best, centuries ago (6th Century BCE) when he noted that when the best leaders have finished their work the people will say "we did it ourselves." (See box)

"A leader is best when people barely know he (sic) exists, when his work is done, his aim fulfilled, they will say: we did it ourselves."
Lao Tzu (604BC – 531BC)

2. Trust the Process. The process always arrives at a solution, even if it is not what the facilitator thought it would be. Often that may mean that the group gets stuck and cannot see its way forward. It can be tempting for the facilitator to want to jump in and rescue or suggest a solution. That can rob the group of some important learning and may also stifle the possibility of a totally new and creative solution emerging.

3. The Knowledge and Wisdom is Present in the Group. When a group comes together the individuals that make it up bring a range of experiences, understandings, ideas, and skills. Facilitation enables that wisdom and knowledge to be tapped and used by the entire group. A wise facilitator knows that all that is necessary for a creative decision or solution to emerge is already present in the group. If there is anything further needed by the group, then the group has within it the knowledge of where and how to get what it needs.

4. The Less I Say the Better. Related to the first idea, it is better for the facilitator to err on the side of "less is more" and to use silence as a powerful ally. Good facilitation enables all members of the group to contribute and participate in the decision-making process. A useful metaphor for a facilitator to remember is that the facilitator has two eyes, two ears, and one mouth. Hence, a facilitator should be watching and listening to twice as much as they are saying. Silence opens up space into which people can step.

5. Create the Space for Conversation. A cup, mug or bowl are nothing without their space. It is the space inside the cup that holds the purpose for which the cup was designed. So it is with facilitation. A facilitator creates the space within which the purpose of the group coming together takes place. And that purpose? Dialogue. In order for groups to make decisions or solve problems, they must converse. The more that a facilitator can encourage conversation and dialogue among participants, the better.

Five concepts, all inter-related. Any one of these concepts implies the other four and all five together suggest any one of them.

When groups form, whether by chance or by deliberate action, there are two prime needs present in the group – group task needs and the personal needs of each participant. Both are important to the group and it is the facilitator's task to help maintain the balance between these needs. Think of it like a see-saw.

T = Task. P = Personal. M = Maintenance

The facilitator is like the fulcrum in the middle, around which the task needs and personal needs move up and down. As we all know (if we can remember our childhood well) the fun of a see-saw was when it moved up and down, not when it remained at a standstill, or when the weight at one end was so much that the see-saw was unable to move. It is no different with the group dynamic see-saw.

Sometimes the task needs must be paramount, yet at other times the personal needs must be given attention. People form groups in order to create something, achieve a goal or learn something. If that isn't happening then the enthusiasm, motivation or sense of purpose for the participants can dissipate, with the group collapsing from inertia. If personal needs are not met, then people may lose interest and drop out of the group, perhaps taking with them some important skill, knowledge or idea. It has been said that people join a learning group in order to learn something, but that what keeps them there are the relationships that they make. This is no different for a group that has a more external, or social change purpose.

A few of the things that a facilitator needs to be aware of in order to maintain the balance between task and personal needs include:

- Ensuring that all participants are encouraged to participate. This means that the facilitator must be encouraging, have an open and receptive manner and be aware of equity issues. (see the chapter on **Encouraging**)
- An ability to maintain an open and full communication between participants, including the ability to draw out silent members. This means being comfortable with different styles of groups working together (including individual time, pair work, small groups, interactive movement, as well as the more traditional full group discussion).
- Being open to the full range of human expression, including feelings, emotions, and intuition, as well as intellectual expression. This may mean specifically allowing for, or even promoting, the expression of heart and gut "thoughts."
- Helping to relieve tension by recognising the importance of humour (although ensuring that the humour is not of a disrespectful nature – see p 108). The use of ice- breakers and other forms of "time out" activities can be helpful, not just to relieve tension, but also to reduce the possibility of boredom or inattention.

- Reminding the group of their goals and direction. Being able to summarise where a group has got to and then suggesting the next steps, is a useful function of a facilitator.
- Being able to work with disagreement or differences of opinion in a way that respects the individual needs of all yet also recognises the task needs of the group. An understanding of techniques for doing this are useful skills for facilitators to have in their "toolbox."
- Testing for consensus or agreements. This helps groups to recognise when and where progress is being made. If agreements are not reached then it may be necessary to restate the problem, issue, or concern that the group is working on. It is important to summarise the steps that have been made along the way, thus being able to clarify sticking points.
- Most of all, the primary function of a facilitator is to listen. Listen for new ideas, areas of agreement, areas of disagreement, to those who are silent. Listen for signs of restlessness, misunderstandings, or for conversation dominators.

Okay, but how do facilitators do this? The skills and techniques of facilitation have been written about often and there is a large body of manuals, exercises, and resources available online and elsewhere for those who want to pursue this further.

Dynamic Facilitation
In the early 1990s, a form of facilitation that explored the chaotic energies that could emerge from diversity began to be experimented with. Dynamic Facilitation (as it has been called) deliberately steps into the murky waters of randomness, diversity, and chaos within which our lives and the issues we deal with exist. Rather than the facilitator reminding groups of the goals of the group (as noted above) the facilitator of this dynamic process allows whatever arises at the moment to be brought to attention. Instead of there being an agenda (even a group-designed one) Dynamic Facilitation says that

the agenda is whatever is arising at the time, whether that be feelings, thoughts, concerns, solutions, challenges, or perspectives.

Some advocates and trainers of Dynamic Facilitation liken the process to a family or group of friends around a table doing a jigsaw puzzle together.[72] There is no order to which individuals in the group select pieces of the puzzle and fit them into the emerging picture. No-one is claiming that the puzzle has to be solved or completed in a particular order, nor even that one section of the puzzle must be completed before moving to another section. Yet, the puzzle gets completed. From one perspective this is a haphazard, random and chaotic approach. Yet, in the end, an order (the completed jigsaw) emerges.

Dynamic Facilitation has another name: a Choice-Creating Process. Jim Rough, who pioneered this approach, noted that traditional facilitation processes were often about problem-solving or decision-making, whereas Dynamic Facilitation helps participants to bring up all the choices that may arise, whether the choices are ones they are already aware of or ones that arise from what another participant may say. Hence, the process is highly creative and emergent. It does, however, require a highly skilled facilitator – a facilitator that is not only comfortable with chaos but is able to actively search for randomness, uncertainty, and apparent disorder.

The facilitator of a Choice-Creating Process needs to adopt many of the skills of the traditional facilitator, especially those of creative listening, drawing out the input from participants, and recording each contribution as it arises. Instead of seeking consensus or convergence of thinking, the facilitator in this process is deliberately accepting (even eliciting) divergent thinking.

This can sound confrontational. The facilitator in a Choice-Creating Process shifts confrontational situations from the participants to themselves. Thus, instead of two participants getting involved in an argument where one offers a solution and the other challenges that solution, the facilitator will ask that the participants speak to the

---

[72] Zubizarreta, 2015

facilitator. In one case the facilitator will draw out the solution offered and record that under the heading "Solutions." The facilitator will also draw out the criticisms offered and record those under "Challenges." Thus, nothing is rejected, all parts and all perspectives are welcomed, acknowledged and recorded. This way the participants can see the picture that is slowly emerging.

The above is a very brief introduction to the ideas behind Dynamic Facilitation (Choice-Creating). For a fuller explanation the reader is referred to the Dynamic Facilitation website (www.DynamicFacilitation.com)

Encountering Conflict

You will have noticed that Dynamic Facilitation actively searches for divergent thinking and that this may sometimes lead to conflict or confrontation. Also, you will have noticed that one of the five pre-conditions for the Open Space technique is that passion exists "even to the point that conflict may exist" (See p 120). In the Preface, I wrote that if you wish to change the world or at least a little part of it, then you will find others who agree with you. I warned that there would also be those who were antagonistic. I then posed the question: How do you work with those who disagree with you? These references bring us to encountering conflict. How do we best deal with conflict, for conflict will surely exist for activators?

Mark Gerzon is an internationally acclaimed mediator who has worked in some of the most demanding parts of the world, including Kenya, Nepal, Argentina, Saudi Arabia, Israel/Palestine, and China. Working through conflict, Gerzon says, needs to be based on dialogue, which he contrasts with debate, discussion, and conversation. (See box for a brief description of these other forms). Dialogue is not looking for niceness, he says, rather, it is looking for effectiveness. For this dialogue to be effective there appear to be two underlying principles that are required: Trust building, and the setting aside of assumptions. Both of these principles have been touched on elsewhere in this book, but I will briefly re-examine them under this heading.

Trust in conflictual situations is built using five tools:[73]

1. Commitment to seeing the whole conflict (integral vision).
2. Analysing the elements of the conflict and the larger system (or systems) of which it is a part (systems thinking).
3. Being fully present to both the outer reality and your inner experience of it (presence).
4. Asking initial questions that deepen your knowledge of the situation (inquiry).
5. Surveying alternative ways of communicating in order to determine which of them will be most useful (conscious conversation).

Gerzon notes that the assumptions we bring to conflicts (assumptions about ourselves, the others, and the conflict itself) hold the energy that can be transformative when true dialogue takes place.

Debate

To debate means to take a viewpoint and then use your debating skills to defend that point of view and attack that of the opposition. The word debate derives from the Old French word *debatre* – to fight. *De* meaning *down* and *batre* meaning *to beat*. Hence, literally, debate means to beat down.

Discussion

Less antagonistic than debate, nevertheless *discussion* does have an oppositional sense to it. The word shares a common etymology with other English words such as percussion and concussion. Its Latin roots are in the words *dis* meaning *apart* and *quatere* – to shake, smash, scatter, disperse. Thus, discussion means to shake apart.

Conversation

Conversation has a pleasantness about it, a sense of companionship, a feel-good element. Indeed, when we research the roots of this word we find exactly those elements. Again, it is Latin in origin combining the word *com* (*with*) and the word *vetere* (*to turn, to turn about*) giving us the idea of *to turn about with*. For the Latins it connoted the act of living together, having dealings with others. Nice as it may be, conversation is not generally the wellspring of creative new thoughts, ideas or possibilities (although it could be the catalyst for dialogue). It can open up our minds somewhat, but it falls short of "unleashing the power of our imagination."

---

[73] Mark Gerzon,2006

This requires us to examine assumptions that we normally would not shed light on. Some of these assumptions have been discussed earlier in this book – our beliefs, our cultural biases, our stereotypes of others. True dialogue helps us uncover the energy trapped within these assumptions.

Dialogue has the capacity to *"unleash the power of our imagination."*[74] David Bohm (the quantum physicist) described dialogue as a shared pool of meaning that was constantly flowing and evolving giving us deeper levels of understanding. These new understandings, he said, were often unseen before the dialogue was entered into. The Russian philosopher, Mikhail Bakhtin, described the dialogic process as one in which: *"Truth is not born, nor is it to be found inside the head, of an individual person, it is born between people collectively searching for truth, in the process of their dialogic interaction."*

For both theorists then, dialogue involves a shared approach that is based on trust and respect and is aimed at discovering new thoughts, new ideas and the ability to create a new future. The etymology of the word is instructive. It comes from two Greek words: *διά (dia)*, meaning *through, across* or *inter*, and *λέγειν (légein)* meaning *to speak*. From this we get a sense of the speech coming through us and between us, rather than being a possession of any one of us.

Dialogue seeks mutual understanding and searches for options, not winners and losers. It does not look for finality but instead seeks out creative opportunities.

This section has briefly touched on conflict and has suggested that conflict, in context, can be a source of learning, and of opening up creative opportunities. I have deliberately not written about Conflict Resolution or Conflict Management. Readers interested in either of these topics are urged to find the many sources already available online, or in published material.

---

[74] Quote from Stephen Hawking in an advert for British Telecom in 1993

Encountering Nature

In late 2004 I was training for a multi-sport race that included kayaking a 67km stretch of a wild South Island (New Zealand) river. One day I decided to undertake a combination paddle, run, cycle training session. Beginning with the kayak, I paddled out from Sumner beach in Christchurch to the Lyttelton Harbour Heads, a distance of approximately 4 km. Paddling around the heads would be another 2km or so, before a 16km paddle up the length of Lyttelton Harbour to the head of the harbour.

The day was fine and once out past the breakers the sea was gentle and rolling. Paddling towards the heads though, the swell increased to about a metre or so, but not something I was too concerned about as I was paddling a very stable kayak.

Suddenly I found myself surrounded by about half a dozen Hector's Dolphins, one of the smallest marine mammals in the world, at no more than 1.5m in length. The dolphins swam alongside me, occasionally leaping out of the water as if to guide me. It was a magical encounter. Hector's Dolphins are endemic to New Zealand shores and their numbers are decreasing. It is estimated that the population of South Island Hector's Dolphin has reduced by almost three-quarters since 1970, due mainly to inshore fishing.

In the increasing swell of the ocean around the harbour heads, the small pod of dolphins stayed with me, swimming easily alongside or slightly ahead of my kayak prow. Reaching the entrance to Lyttelton Harbour, I changed direction from paddling south to paddling westward into and up the harbour. The sea swell reduced dramatically. Just as suddenly as they arrived, my friendly escort of Hector's Dolphins left. I was left with the distinct feeling that they had decided "he's safe now, he'll be okay. We can let him go."

Through our encounters with other humans, we can learn and create opportunities. The same is true of nature, although it is easy to forget that nature offers us just as much opportunity as do our peers, perhaps more so. At least one study has shown that our creativity can increase by 50% after a four-day tramp (trek, hike) in the wilderness, so long as we don't take any social-media technology with us.[75]

In our hectic, busy lives of social change work, it can be easy to forget not only the importance of nature but also our utter reliance on natural systems. Stop and ponder for a moment upon two of the most fundamental ways in which we interact with nature. When we breathe we are providing our bodies with the oxygen that is essential to our lives. If we stop and bring our attention to the breath for even a moment we can begin to connect with this vast natural system. The air we breathe is essential to all life on earth, it helps in the pollination of crops, it allows the water cycle to operate, it helps to maintain the earth's temperature, and it is the medium through which sound travels. Without this last function much of our human-to-human encountering would be next to impossible.

The other natural system that we interact with daily is the water system. Without water, we would be dead within a few days, yet we can take it for granted. Water too is, like air, essential for most forms of life on earth; it transports the nutrients necessary for plant life (including crops), it has been the medium through which much of humankind has transported goods, it is home for approximately one-quarter of the earth's living species. The hydrological cycle is perhaps one of the most well-known and well understood of all natural cycles. So, as with our breath, when we drink a glass of water, think for a moment about that simple encounter, yet realise the enormity of what it signifies.

So we do not have to go off on ten-day wilderness experiences, or climb to the highest peak, or spend a couple of hours meditating beneath a tree. We can encounter nature by being mindful of our breathing, and our drinking of water. But, if we do make the time and put in the effort to deliberately encounter nature in more explorative ways, then we will learn much about nature and ourselves. Doing so may be getting more imperative, especially if we are to learn

---

[75] Atchley RA, Strayer DL, Atchley p. 2012

how to address the multi-emergencies mentioned at the beginning of this book.

Humans began striding the earth approximately 200,000 years ago and for the most part have been integral and co-operative players in the natural systems of the earth. Around 5,000 years ago that began to change so that culture began to predominate over nature. The beginning of the Industrial Revolution in the mid-18th century exacerbated that alienation from nature. Bill Plotkin, an eco-psychologist, claims that *"our lives have become increasingly less attuned to nature and more solely to culture. Because of this, many modern cultures have diverged from their origins in nature, resulting in billions of modern lives radically alienated from the natural world and cultures devoid of the integrity and survival value implicit in natural systems. "*[76]

This alienation has become so severe that there is now a term for it – Nature Deficit Disorder. The term was coined in 2005 by the American author Richard Louv in a book that not only recorded the growing alienation but also offered the benefits of encountering nature.[77] In that book, Louv was addressing his concerns primarily to children. Later however, upon being challenged by a woman in

> **Quotes from Richard Louv**
> *"For a new generation, nature is more abstraction than reality. Increasingly, nature is something to watch, to consume, to wear—to ignore."*
>
> *"Yet, at the very moment that the bond is breaking between the young and the natural world, a growing body of research links our mental, physical, and spiritual health directly to our association with nature—in positive ways. Several of these studies suggest that thoughtful exposure of youngsters to nature can even be a powerful form of therapy for attention-deficit disorders and other maladies. As one scientist puts it, we can now assume that just as children need good nutrition and adequate sleep, they may very well need contact with nature."*

---

[76] Plotkin, Bill. 2008.
[77] Louv, Richard. 2005

Seattle who told him *"Listen to me, adults have nature deficit disorder too,"* he wrote a follow-up book, *The Nature Principle,* to acknowledge this and to show how by tapping into natural systems we can boost our mental acuity, enhance creativity, restore our well-being and, ultimately, build healthier, more sustainable communities and societies.

Joanna Macy is another writer, systems thinker and Buddhist scholar who has given much thought to how we can encounter nature in affirming, exploratory and learning ways. Her manual, *Coming Back To Life,*[78] describes no less than 60 practices for; opening our hearts to the pain of disengagement; opening our eyes to see what is happening, and encountering nature with gratitude and openness. She calls it the *Work that Reconnects,* or *The Great Turning* – a term that Bill Plotkin and others also use.

All these guides, mentors and teachers firmly place encountering nature as central to their practice. Human development cannot proceed without being intimately connected with nature. Indeed, Plotkin's model of the human psychological journey is ecocentric because, as he says, *"(nature) informs and guides every chosen step of our maturation, if we let it."* Those last four words – *if we let it* – are crucial. Our encounters with nature must be authentic, honest and transparent.

What do we discover when we honestly encounter nature, and if we are open to let it inform and guide us? We discover at least seven learnings:

- Natural systems are self-organising. There is no hierarchic order with command centres, organising or authorising mechanisms. Nature adapts and self-regulates.
- Nature nurtures new life, often from the ashes, embers or debris of old life. It is cyclic and ever evolving.
- Nature is cooperative. This may sound nonsensical when we think of the term "survival of the fittest." But, when Charles Darwin borrowed that phrase he did not have in mind the idea

---

[78] Macy, Joanna & Brown, Molly. 2014

of fitness meaning strongest or fastest and did not conceive it in a hierarchic manner. Nature is a community wherein there is a place for all, rather than a conglomeration of individuals all competing for limited space. (see also p 112)

- Nature is a system with all parts co-dependent, co-arising, and co-existing.
- Nature is full of potential and all parts of natural systems are continually developing or reaching towards their potential.
- In natural systems there is no waste. Everything is used, reused and recycled. There is no overconsumption. If there are brief times of over-consumption, natures self-organising principle kicks in to re-stabilise the system.

This all sounds wonderful, doesn't it? Nature – the idyllic, utopian playground where everything is calm, rosy, free, and accommodating. It isn't, and most of us know that. It can be dangerous, it doesn't easily accept fools and it certainly doesn't take sides. None of which contradicts the seven learnings above. The point is that nature is a system. Our cultural bias is to view reality through our individual eyes, from our personal sense of self. This cultural bias is exactly the reason that encountering nature is vital to our understanding of how we respond to the multi-emergencies. By encountering nature our sense of self begins to dissipate, we begin to *"step out of self-deception"* as one author has put it.[79]

When we step out of self-deception and encounter nature, we allow more creative opportunities to emerge. Wandering in nature helps us make that step.

The ecopsychologist and wilderness guide, Bill Plotkin,[80] is a strong advocate of wandering in nature. In his eight-stage model of the human development journey, he claims that wandering in nature is one of the developmental activities that, ideally, every late adolescent would undertake. Sadly, most adults in our western-styled culture do

---

[79] Smith, Rodney. 2010.
[80] Plotkin, Bill. op cit.

not get to experience this (although it is never too late[81]) and hence do not journey through this stage of the eco-centric developmental journey. Plotkin notes that the importance of nature wandering is that, *"the wanderer seeks the hidden, the mysterious, the wild. (The wanderer) knows that the changes in consciousness and identity that (are gone) through while searching are as important as finding what is being sought. The wanderer is not in a hurry. Wandering is as valuable as anything else the wanderer might do."*

That final phrase bears repeating: *"Wandering is as valuable as anything else the wanderer might do."* Indeed so. It is our disconnect from nature, from the Earth, from the natural rhythms of life, and from the very system that nourishes us that could arguably be claimed to be the primary cause of many of the emergencies with which this book began.

Finally, a quick mention of what encountering nature is not. Visiting a zoo or an aquarium is not what is being advocated here in terms of encountering nature. Visiting zoos and aquaria is much like going to an art gallery. We visit the gallery, look at a painting for a while, maybe ponder it and then move on to the next one. We continue doing that as we move around the gallery, and after an hour or two we leave. We may have seen some exceptional art, we may have learnt a little about a particular artist or genre of art, but we have not encountered the art. We have not immersed ourselves in it. We haven't entered the artist's studio and gotten ourselves splattered in paint, or experienced the deft brush strokes that slowly bring to life the painting in its entirety. It is much the same with zoos and aquaria. We see some animals in unnatural settings, either behind bars or glass panels, and we do so from the safety of a human-designed environment. Whether the reader finds zoos to be ethical or unethical is not the point. The point here is that zoo and aquarium visits are not the meaning behind encountering nature that is encouraged in this book.

Here are a few ideas for encountering nature:

---

[81] I used to own a T-shirt that read *"It's never too late to have a happy childhood."*

- Take a walk along a beach. Smell the salty air. Wade in the surf. Feel the sand beneath your feet. Watch the seabirds swirl and dive. Try *tiger walking* – walk purposively placing one foot down with the heel striking first, rolling onto the outside of the foot, with the little toe grounding, followed by the other toes in turn, with your big toe being the last part of the foot to touch the sand. Then repeat with the other foot.
- Garden. Plant herbs and research not only their culinary benefits but also their medicinal ones. Notice how the seasons and the growth of plants interact.
- Go hiking (tramping, trekking) in the woods, the mountains, the forests and the river beds. Take your food and accommodation with you and spend at least 3 days without any contact with civilisation.
- Sit on a hilltop at sunrise or sunset and watch the sun rise or set. Watch the colours in the sky change and merge into one another. At sunset watch the flocks of birds return to their nesting places. At sunrise feel the warmth of the sun slowly increase.
- Find a quiet place at night away from urban lights and just stare at the stars. If you look for long enough you'll see a meteor (shooting star) – you should see one approximately every 10 – 15 minutes, more often during "meteor showers."
- Combine the last two of these suggestions and spend the whole night, from sunset to sunrise, outside, beneath the stars. Watch as those stars slowly revolve above you. Contemplate your place in the cosmos. Consider that the light from the nearest star (not counting our own – the Sun) takes four and a half years to reach us. For many stars the light has taken hundreds, even thousands of years to reach us. You are literally looking backward in time. Can you pick out the planets? Can you identify the constellations?[82]

---

[82] Find out how indigenous people think of the stars. Perhaps it is a quite different concept. For example in Australia one of the "constellations" identified by the

- Take a trip to a waterfall, stand underneath and feel the water splashing and caressing your body. Take a dip in the pool at the bottom of the waterfall. Revel in the invigorating coolness of the water.
- Get some flippers, mask, and snorkel and find a lagoon, sheltered beach or a lake. Without the use of compressed air, explore the underwater domain. Are there fish, coral or kelp in the area? How is this underwater environment different to the above water environment?
- Climb a tree and sit on a limb watching the birdlife and other creatures that use the tree for habitat, food or as a transport network. As you sit there, ponder how this tree connects with the rest of the local ecosystem. How extensive are its roots? Where do the nutrients come from? What's going on in the leaves?
- With a partner try this variation on the Trust Walk idea. Find a non-urban environment and take turns being led with eyes closed, in silence. Your partner guides you with their arm or hand. Your partner finds and guides you to an experience – it could be the bark of a tree, a fragrant flower, a group of pebbles or the sound of a bird twittering. When your guide stops they will gently move your head so that you are facing the experience they have decided on. Your guide then says "Open your eyes and look in the mirror." The idea is to see things in a new light as if you were looking in a mirror for the first time.[83]
- Try walking meditation. Kick off your shoes or sandals, step out of your socks, and walk with gentle, and slow, steps upon the earth. Feel the grass, sand, dirt, or rock beneath your feet. Become aware of the earth beneath you. Is it cold, is it warm, what is the texture? Do you feel connected to the earth?

Guringai people is the "Great Emu" which is identified by dark nebulae, and not by stars at all.

[83] This exercise (called the Mirror Walk) is one of many suggested by Joanna Macy.

To really extend your encounters with nature you might like to opt for one of these:

- Spend time on an organic farm. World Wide Opportunities on Organic Farms (WWOOF)[84] helps put volunteers in touch with farmers. The volunteer works on the farm in return for accommodation, food and the opportunity to learn about organic farming.
- Book a guided wilderness experience. There are numerous organisations offering such experiences. Find one that offers an experience based on integrity. Ideally, you want an organisation that is guided as much by the heart as it is by the profit motive.
- Of course you don't have to find and pay for a guide. You could do it yourself and go off for a month or more into a remote area that is unconnected to civilisation. Make you own shelter, become a "hunter and gatherer," cook your own food, spend time contemplating your surroundings. For inspiration read *My Year Without Matches*[85] by Claire Dunn, an Australian woman who *"disillusioned and burnt out by her job, quits a comfortable life to spend a year off the grid in a wilderness survival program."*

Encountering Self

It may seem surprising to find that the role of the self in all this is not addressed until near the end. Perhaps so, yet once we have worked through and come to fully appreciate the implications of the **COFFEE** acronym we discover that the sense of self is implicit within, and we have been encountering self through all facets of the acronym.

Self and the sense of self-hood has been the pursuit of philosophers, religious teachers, psychologists, and spiritual seekers for millennia. The self has been the theme of numerous novels,

---

[84] WWOOF originally meant Working Weekends On Organic Farms and began in England in 1971. See http://www.wwoof.net
[85] Dunn, Claire. 2014

poems, essays, and dramatic performances since the written word was invented. The world is full of myths, legends, and stories proclaiming the pursuit of self and the place of the self in cosmology. It is not my intention to add to this vast repertoire. Some comments arising from a consideration of the **COFFEE** approach are in order, however.

Within the **COFFEE** acronym, the middle two words (Flow From) are pertinent to a consideration of self. If we stop to think about our self then we will eventually discover that our self is an emergent one. Our self flows from a myriad of phenomena, circumstances, and the actions of others. Think for a moment about your moment of creation. Of the millions of sperm that swam towards your mother's ovum, it was just that one that fertilised the egg to begin the creation of you. How would you, your life, your self, have been different if it had been another one of those millions of sperm that got there first? Whether you believe this was randomness, chance, divine intervention, fate, or some larger purpose is not what I am seeking to look at here. It is simply that you are here because of one amongst millions of possibilities. Looking back on our lives we can see if we seriously search, that at many points in our lives (perhaps even at every moment) we are emerging from a swirling, infinite cloud of possibilities. Where you were born, who your parents were (maybe even if you had parents), the culture you were born into, the pool of brothers, sisters, cousins, aunts, uncles, neighbours, all played a part in who you were and who you are becoming. Our self is never constant, it is continuously emerging.

So it is when we work with the idea of **COFFEE.** Our creativity helps to shape who we are. In the creative process of writing this book I have changed who I am. My understandings have changed, my view of the world has changed, my relationships with others have changed. I have emerged through that process. When we open up to opportunities our self will emerge from each and every one of those opportunities. If we pass up an opportunity our self is different than had we taken up the opportunity. When I act in encouraging ways, or I am encouraged, then I change. Just look at the face of a child when they are encouraged. Their face lights up, they beam.   Contrast that with a child who is not encouraged.   The encouragement has changed them – their self-hood has emerged from that encouragement. Finally, who we encounter undoubtedly moulds us in some way, even if only in subtle ways. Some of our encounters, though, can be monumentally life and self-changing.

Hence, our self is not an unchanging, set-in-concrete identity. Our self is continually changing, adapting, evolving, growing – it is emerging. The self is an emergent process.

The second implication that can be drawn out of all the previous pages is that each self is located in an intricate, complex, network of inter-connected and mutually arising phenomena. When we inquire into this complexity one thing that becomes very obvious is that the sense of an independent, separate self dissolves before our eyes (ironic as that may sound). This is not to say that there is no-self, as some would assert. What it means is that there is no self that stands alone, no self that is unaffected by other "selves" (human and non-human), no self that has an existence in and of itself. The implications of this are enormous for our selves and for the manner in which we approach the emergencies that this book began with.   Looked at simplistically, each of us (each self) contributes to the creation of those emergencies, as well as contributing to repairing the harm that these emergencies do. Furthermore, each of these emergencies helps to create our self. We cannot help but be affected by them, whether we watch the news or not. Ignorance does not indemnify us from the effects.

Rene Descartes, in the 17th century, gave us the famous phrase *je pense, donc je suis – I think, therefore I am.* This phrase has often been quoted and alluded to, almost ironically, without thinking. The phrase supposedly proves our existence as well as solidifying the idea of the self as the one and only reality. This sense of self became the over-arching one in western societies over the following three hundred years. Descartes notion, however, is now coming to be questioned and replaced by other ideas of the self. Some of these ideas come from within western culture, others from cultures outside the western one.

The Zulu concept of *ubuntu* is especially vivid. Desmond Tutu describes *ubuntu* as:[86] *"the philosophy and belief that a person is only a person through other people. In other words, we are human only in relation to other humans. Our humanity is bound up in one another... This interconnectedness is the very root of who we are."*

The concept is not confined to the Zulu; it occurs in many African cultures and is notably different to the western notion. *Ubuntu* describes a notion of who I am as being so intertwined with others and the environment that any idea of an independent self disappears.

A very similar concept is found within Asian thought and philosophy. One such is the term *interbeing* – a term coined by the Vietnamese Buddhist monk Thich Nhat Hanh. Thich Nhat Hanh describes the concept as being *"the many in the one and the one containing the many."* In a nod to Descartes, Thich Nhat Hanh expresses interbeing as:[87] *"I am, therefore you are. You are, therefore I am. We inter-are."*

This sense of the self being intricately interconnected with other selves, so much so that the idea of a separate self evaporates, is at odds with the traditional western view. Thich Nhat Hanh extends the interconnection beyond the human realm so that the whole non-human realm is included in constructing the self. His concept of the self is one of ecocentrism.

Okay, okay, enough of the metaphysical rambling. Each of us still retains a self or at least some sense of self, and each of us contemplates that in our own unique way. In the context of this book, I wish to consider the self in terms of what is healthy and what is unhealthy when it comes to how we approach the emergencies and how we work with emergence. The previous sub-section (encountering nature) is important in this sense. Understanding our place in nature, and our part in the enormous network, a healthy self

---

[86] Desmond and Mpho Tutu, 2014
[87] Thich Nhat Hanh, 1987

may be considered to be one that is eco-centric. An unhealthy self, on the other hand, can be considered to be one that is ego-centric.[88]

In constructing our sense of self we are shaped by our culture and society. In turn, we help to co-create our culture. We are born into our society and culture. If we consider our culture to be a healthy one then we will act in conforming ways and seek to sustain our culture. If on the other hand, we consider our culture to be unhealthy we will act in ways that attempt to transform it. If we live in a healthy culture then we are likely to form a healthy self. If our culture is an unhealthy one then to construct a healthy self becomes a difficult, but not impossible, task. Those of you who have read this far into this book undoubtedly recognise unhealthy aspects of the society into which you were born. You have a desire to transform that society, to co-create a more mature, healthier, one.

In the process of transformation of society we must encounter our self. We must encounter who we are, because a healthy society cannot be created by unhealthy selves, nor can a healthy society be created by "healthy" conformists.[89]

When we consider the nature of the emergencies facing us, and we consciously and fully encounter our self, we discover that our self becomes increasingly shaped by something more than our society. Many of the emergencies we face are environmental in nature. As we enquire into who we are we find that our place in nature has a significant influence on our sense of self. We move from a sense of self that is centred on the ego to one that is eco-centric.

---

[88] I am indebted here to the writings of Bill Plotkin, an eco and soul-centred psychologist based in the US. Bill's three books, *Nature and the Human Soul, Soulcraft,* and *Wild Mind* are highly recommended reading. Bill's writings clearly identify the difference between an eco-centric psychology and an ego-centric psychology.

[89] By "healthy" conformist I mean a self that has accepted "unhealthy" society and has managed to adjust their self so as to conform to that society's expectations, norms, mores and rules. See for example Bill Plotkin, *Nature and the Human Soul,* New World Library, Novato, California, 2008

As our inter-connected, eco-centric self, unfolds we become more visionary, more creative. Being able to see and understand the connected wholeness of life provides us with the ability to tap into the sort of creativity that Albert Einstein was talking about. (See p 31 and pp 54-55)

So, how do we go about encountering our self? How do we open up our sense of self, so that we are no longer constrained by an ego-centric self, but by a far more encompassing, fuller self? Many of the techniques, skills, and experiences already covered in this book allow this to occur, even if encountering our self was not the intention at the time. Here are a few ideas (some already covered in previous pages):

Listening to our intuition. In the chapter on Creativity, we heard Miriam-Rose Ungunmeer's description of deep inner listening and how that makes us whole again. (See pp 41) Listening to our intuition provides us with a connection to our self, especially our deeper self, towards soul.

Nurturing our compassion. Compassion has been the subject of much research recently showing that our well-being is enhanced by acts of giving and showing compassion. The neuroscience of this suggests that we connect the pleasure of others with our own pleasure centres. Our sense of self is founded, at least in part, by recognising our common humanity. The Dalai Lama has succinctly summarised this, *"If you want others to be happy, practice compassion. If you want to be happy, practice compassion."*

Fostering empathy. In the chapter on Encouraging we saw that by becoming more self-aware we are in a better position to be able to empathise with others. (See pp 86-94) It is not a one-way street, however. Empathising with others assists us to become more self-aware. It is a win-win exercise.

Wandering in, and encountering nature. The sub-section, Encountering Nature, talked about the importance of wandering in nature with Bill Plotkin being quoted as suggesting that wandering is as important as anything else the wanderer may do. (See pp 138-139) Wandering in nature, according to Plotkin, is essential for

"Westerners who have wandered so far from nature." He goes on to state that, *"What nature has to say is the necessary complement to what we hear all day long from news, ads, and social chatter. To save our souls, we need nature's news."*

Meditation was introduced in the chapter titled From. (See p 84). A number of benefits were mentioned there with one being that of releasing the mind from clutter, clatter, and chatter. A mind that is not distracted by this constant chatter allows our consciousness to become clearer, more settled, opening up for us a pathway towards a deeper understanding of our self.

Encouraging others. When we act in ways that are encouraging to others we find that we become encouraged also. Both of us are en-heartened and in that process we discover something of our selves. To encourage others we have to become attentive and present. In being present we notice not only the other person or persons, we also notice more of ourselves. (See pp 101-103)

Developing our creative listening abilities. In order to be able to creatively listen to others, it is necessary for us to be self-aware. Fortunately, the process involved in listening creatively to someone else provides us with the opportunity to listen to ourselves. We discover ourselves in the process of creatively listening. Creative listening, self- awareness and listening to our self are all part of a flowing co-creative act. (See pp 95-98)

The emergencies that we face may themselves be catalysts for discovering our eco-selves. These emergencies may just be the collective kick that we need. Joanna Macy suggests that when we face these emergencies our old sense of self erodes. She says that this is, *"Because once we stop denying the crises of our time and let ourselves experience the depth of our own responses to the pain of our world whether it is the burning of the Amazon rainforest, the famines of Africa, or the homeless in our own cities the grief or anger or fear we experience cannot be reduced to concerns for our own individual skin. We are capable of suffering with our world, and that is the true meaning of compassion. It enables us to recognize our profound interconnectedness with all beings. Don't ever apologize for crying for the trees burning in the Amazon or over the waters polluted from mines in the Rockies. Don't apologize for the sorrow, grief, and rage you feel. It is a measure of your humanity and your maturity. It is a measure of your open heart, and as your heart breaks open there will be room for the world to heal. "*[90]

In Macy's view developing an eco-centric self does not require an altruistic, virtuous nobility by each of us. All that is needed is a willingness to be present to our own pain and the suffering of the world.

---

[90] Joanna Macy, *The Greening of the Self,* filmsforaction.org/articles/the-greening-of-the-self/ accessed 2 November 2016.

XII
THE WHOLE BREW

How do you make a cup of coffee? Me, I put some water in a kettle, boil it, then pour it over a teaspoon of instant coffee in a mug and add milk. My local barista answers this question in a more sophisticated manner and with more passion. Neither answer fully explores the complexity of making a cup of coffee though. Consider the process all the way from the growing of the coffee bean to the steaming cup of coffee in front of you. Since an Ethiopian goat herder first discovered coffee, the cultivation of coffee plants has spread throughout the world. To grow the plant requires the proper soil conditions, nutrients, sunshine, rain and/or irrigation. Numerous ingredients go together to allow the coffee to be grown. The crop is planted, tended and harvested by, often peasant, farmers. Once harvested think of the dozens, possibly hundreds, of hands through which the bean passes to get to your local café. Farmers, truck drivers, forklift operators, ship owners and operators, customs officials, more truck drivers. It may not even be possible to count them all. There are those who roast the bean, those who package it, the café owners, storekeepers, the banks that help fund coffee enterprises, and finally the barista. That's just the coffee, what about the container, the mug that it gets poured into? Maybe it was made by a potter, or perhaps by a production worker in a factory somewhere. Where did the materials for the mug come from? Then, think even wider. What about the parents of all those people, their teachers, other family members, their friends. All play a part (albeit some only slight) in the making of a cup of coffee.

The complexity and diversity behind a cup of coffee is immeasurable. When it comes to addressing the multi-emergencies the complexity is even more so. The **COFFEE** acronym does not specifically state it, but inherent in the acronym's approach is that in order to address the complexity of these emergencies we must embrace diversity. None of us can fully understand any of the emergencies, let alone the myriad connections between them. If we cannot understand them on our own, then our individual ability to find solutions is close to non-existent. We need our diversity. We need the experience, background, knowledge, skills and wisdom that only tapping into our diversity provides.

Therein lies yet another emergency: dwindling diversity. We are losing biodiversity at an alarming rate. We are also losing our cultural diversity through globalisation. And the two, biodiversity and cultural diversity loss, are connected. The World Wildlife Fund (WWF) in the Netherlands published a sobering piece of research in 2004 that showed that biodiversity loss and cultural diversity loss parallel each other and that one influences the other.[91] The researchers tracked species extinction as a proxy for biodiversity loss and language loss as a proxy for cultural diversity loss.

The study noted that there was a strong geographical correlation between biodiversity and language diversity. In those parts of the world with high biodiversity (mostly central and northern South America, tropical Africa, Asia and Borneo and New Guinea)[92] there is also a high level of language diversity. At the other end of the spectrum, those areas with low biodiversity (Canada, Scandinavia, northern China and Russia) also show very low language diversity.

What was particularly disturbing about the study was that, since 1970, in most parts of the world the decline of species and the loss of language have both undergone a similar rate of depletion (around 30%.) In North America and Europe, as the authors explain, most of the species extinction had already occurred prior to 1970 and so those areas did not show such a dramatic decline since the 1970s.

The decline in both instances (nature and culture) is attributable to similar causes: human population growth and mobility, increased consumption, and globalisation. At the confluence of these two losses of diversity is a threat. Some would argue that surely it is

---

[91] Loh, Jonathan & Harmon, David. 2004.

[92] Interestingly, these are also the geographical locations of most of the coffee growing regions on the planet.

better if the human population all spoke just one language, in order to ease communication. But, as the authors of this study point out, when we lose language diversity we lose with it the accumulated knowledge of local ecosystems. We lose an understanding of local species and phenomena. We lose indigenous knowledge of how to live with natural eco-systems.

Thus, it is important that we not only use our diversity, but we also protect it.

Diversity brings with it not only a greater source of knowledge and experience but also a source of tension. In diversity there will be divergences of opinion, differing ways of looking at the world. The social change activator needs to be aware of this and not get side-tracked into thinking that these differences mean that a collective response is not possible.

Hence, one of the attributes of an activator in the 21st century is that of adaptability and flexibility. The activator needs to be able to work amongst the turbulence and conflict that seems to be going on. An understanding of emergence is helpful – it tells us that below the surface of tension and conflict there is an order that is working itself out, that will emerge if we let it. All chaotic systems go through a period of turbulence before a new order is created. Indeed, some chaotic systems fluctuate wildly just before settling down into a new sense of order.

Brewing the COFFEE

Now we get to the exciting part. What happens when we take each of the words of the acronym – **COFFEE** – and brew them together and serve them all at once? That is how all acronyms and this one is no exception, should be treated – as a whole, as a complete idea. Acronyms are one of the simplest and most common forms of mnemonic – an aid to memory. The **COFFEE** acronym presented in this book is simply a way to remember a way of thinking, especially for those who wish to bring about social change or undertake community development.

Neither the **COFFEE** acronym - nor this book itself - offer a step-by-step, linear process. Reading this has not provided you with a "how to" manual for bringing about social change, or community development. Far from it. If anything, this book suggests that step-by-step, "how-to" processes are unlikely to work. They are unlikely to work because they rely upon control. They rely, further, on a mindset that believes that all parts of a system can be understood and that the actions of the various components of the system can be accurately predicted in advance. What is presented here is simply a way to think about what you do, how you do it, and who you do it with - whatever "it" may be.

The other feature to note about this acronym is that each of the words making it up can individually be explored and our understanding of them deepened. However, it is when the six components of the acronym are brought together, and we work from an understanding of the whole, that something unseen, unknown, or unpredictable may emerge. This is in keeping with one of the early ideas presented in this book – the concept and process of emergence.

COFFEE reminds us that instead of trying to bring about change from a top-down, hierarchic, linear, mechanistic planning approach, what we need to do is constantly be aware of the opportunities that arise from many and every encounter. It reminds us that everyone we meet is an expert and has something of value to add to conversations. It reminds us that in order to allow creative opportunities to emerge we need to be encouraging, and not quick to judge, dismiss or dispute ideas. It reminds us that, if we allow it, a single conversation or a large workshop can be a container for new ideas. It reminds us that we need to create the space within which conversations can flow. It reminds us that we, collectively, co-create our environment and our reality.

COFFEE challenges us to think of our desire to change the world. This book began by suggesting that there were a number of emergencies that we wanted to solve or fix in some way. **COFFEE** asks us to be mindful of our encounters with one another and with nature and to approach these encounters in encouraging ways. When we do we may be astonished at the entirely new ways of thinking and perceiving that are opened up. One very challenging understanding that this approach points to is our unhelpful desire to solve things. Just as women have been asking men for decades to not offer advice or try to fix things, but to just listen, so too has the western cultural approach been to rush in and try to fix things. Indeed, the emergencies that we have today are, by and large, a result of our wanting to fix things. The **COFFEE** acronym suggests that we abandon that approach and replace it with creative listening and encouragement so as to allow creative opportunities to flow from the space between us.

COFFEE also reminds us that we are living in systems. In many ways, we can think of ourselves as a living system living within systems (e.g. families and neighbourhoods), that in turn are contained within larger systems (cultures, nation-states etc.), and all these are surrounded by the even larger Earth eco-system and beyond that to the galactic and cosmic systems. This is not simple mystical or impractical thinking. Often it is our collective inability to think in terms of systems that has led to the interconnected emergencies that began this book.

A Systems View

Systems thinking is a way of looking at and thinking about things that contain a number of parts that are interconnected to achieve or do something. That is a fairly simple definition, but you will see that within it there are three main ideas.

1. A system has parts, or elements.
2. The parts of the system are connected to one another in some way, sometimes obvious, sometimes not so obvious, and sometimes even hidden.
3. The system has a purpose, it does something. It is important to note that we may not be able to discern what that purpose is, yet we intuitively know there is one.

Take your body as an example of a system. It has many parts; bones, skin, organs, muscles, ligaments, blood. It includes all the tiny parts such as cells, DNA, mitochondria. These are all connected. Most of us don't even stop to think of how everything is connected. But if you take a moment now and think about it, I guarantee that you will not be able to think of a part of your body that is not connected, and in some way dependent upon, other parts. What is the purpose of all these inter-connected parts? You! The living, breathing, thinking, sensing you. The primary purpose of all those parts connecting with one another is to keep you alive.

That is basically what systems are. **COFFEE** reminds us to be aware of systems. It reminds us to think of the way in which parts of systems are connected to achieve something. In this case, the parts are each of the words (**C**reative, **O**pportunities, **F**low, **F**rom, **E**ncouraging, **E**ncounters). As you read through the previous pages you will have noticed the connections between these parts (e.g. how creativity is enhanced by encouragement, or how we may discover an opportunity in a chance encounter). The purpose of the acronym is to provide us with a simply remembered mnemonic for a way of thinking systematically.

One of the world's leading systems thinkers, Donella Meadows, gave a lot of thought to many of the emergencies noted in this book and also to the best ways to intervene in systems. Meadows was the lead researcher in the ground-breaking study *The Limits to Growth*,[93] published in 1972. The study was groundbreaking for two reasons. It was the first time that the power of computers was used to model human systems. In doing so, it became one of the first studies to put forward scenarios that showed that we could not continue *business-as-usual* in a finite world.

The last book written (published posthumously[94]) by Meadows was devoted specifically to systems thinking. In it Meadows attempted to find what she called the leverage points in a

---

[93] Meadows, Meadows, Randers & Behrens III, 1972.
[94] Meadows, Donella H. 2008.

system. In other words, what are the most effective ways to *"change the structure of systems to produce more of what we want and less of that which is undesirable."*

Meadows considered twelve possible leverage points, ranging from changing the parts of the system through to changing the paradigm that created the system. Unsurprisingly, she suggested that changing the parts was the least effective. The most effective, but not necessarily easy to do, is to influence the paradigm that enables systems to exist. That means changing the way we think. Human systems arise out of mindsets, worldviews, ideologies, or cultural imperatives. From these paradigms, the goals, structures, rules and parameters of all human systems arise.

We can do that. We can transcend worldviews or ideologies and find different ways to think about how we behave and how we interact with others, with our environment, and with our world.

This book and acronym present one possible way of thinking about how we approach community development, social change and even our own individual deeds and actions. When we think holistically, from a systems perspective, and recognise the phenomenon of emergence, then addressing the multi-faceted emergencies becomes possible.

When we give up on our collective desires for control, when we dismantle our hierarchies, when we overcome our fear of others, then new opportunities arise.

When we understand the Butterfly Effect, when we appreciate complexity, when we embrace our common humanity, then we begin to live in a world of wonder and true development of the human and non-human capabilities.

When we let go of our self-identification, when we learn to listen, when we speak openly, honestly and from a soul-centred perspective, then we just may find that **C**reative **O**pportunities can **F**low **F**rom **E**ncouraging **E**ncounters. We can have our **COFFEE** and drink it too.

Warning, warning, warning

But, hang on. A word or two of warning. Before you begin to think that everything is straight forward and that so long as everyone has their **COFFEE,** just as suggested here, everything will work out well, and that the outcomes we want will emerge, then be warned; it may not turn out that way. Let me return to a discussion about emergence. You will recall that an emergent system includes the following aspects:

- It is unpredictable,
- It is self-organising, and arises from the myriad connections in the system,
- It is much greater than the sum of its parts,
- It is complex,
- It is self-learning and adaptive.

It is apparent, from these aspects, that there are no guarantees, there are no certainties. There are only possibilities. If we apply a **COFFEE** approach, then maybe we will get the outcomes we desire. Maybe we won't. We just have to live with that, we have to acknowledge that. We also have to admit that even when we attempt to do what we consider to be right, we may end up being one of the triggering factors in an outcome that we do not want. Alan Clements[95] put it well when he commented that, *"We must live with the anxiety of an unpredictable world, where the unthinkable often happens."*

---

[95] Clements, Alan. 2003

Whatever action we take in the world has an effect. The final outcome is partly due to our action, but also, due to the actions of dozens, perhaps thousands, or even millions of others. Consequently, whatever we do there is the chance that things do not turn out how we intend them – *no matter* what our intention. Indeed, by trying to change the world in positive ways we run the risk of ending in disaster at the worst or no change at all. (See box for an example).

Is this a reason for sitting back, not acting, or withdrawing from the world? Not at all. Humans seem hard-wired to desire a better life - a life of harmony, fulfilment and contentment. If you are reading this then you are most likely someone who thinks that the current system and structures do not enable life to be the best that it could be, if not personally, then for millions of others. You, like many thousands of others, want to change the world, or at least the way in which your family works. And, so you should. However, the warning here is that we can never know for certain what the outcome will be, and we can surely never know if the outcome will be a beneficial one or a harmful one. But what we can do is act with an intention that our actions will be carried out from an honest, humane and genuine inner heart and soul. Working with **COFFEE**

> **An Example of Things Not Going to Plan**
>
> The introduction of non-native species to an area is an excellent example of positive intentions ending in difficulty, and most of us can cite such instances. In my own country, New Zealand, gorse (Ulex europaeus) was introduced from Europe in the early 1800s because it was thought that it would, as it did in Europe, provide the material for hedges. In fact, in the 1850s a government regulation was introduced requiring that Crown land leased to smallholders be fenced using gorse or hawthorn. Indeed, it is a good hedge in its homeland, but it took to the temperate New Zealand climate with a vigour unknown in northern Europe. Today, it is a highly invasive weed covering 5% of New Zealand's agricultural land.
> Today, there are experiments taking place to work with gorse as a medium for native species to rejuvenate. It remains however, a nightmare to many farmers.

provides us with a way of thinking about how we act that is more honest, humane, and genuine.

One person who knew that we must continue to act for good, no matter the outcome, was Václav Havel, the last president of Czechoslovakia and then the first president of the Czech Republic. Havel was a vocal critic of the communist regime, an advocate of direct democracy, an environmentalist and humanitarian as well as being a poet, philosopher, and writer. He was jailed numerous times by the secret police, before finally leading his country into a new phase. In one of his books, he declared that [96] *"Hope, in the deep and meaningful sense ... is an ability to work for something because it is good, not just because it stands a chance to succeed."*

Havel's words echo those of Thomas Merton, a Trappist monk who came to a similar realisation twenty-four years earlier. Not only was Merton a Catholic monk, he was also committed to nonviolence as a means towards peace and justice. In 1966, at the height of the Vietnam war, a peace activist, Jim Forest, wrote to Merton telling him of his despair and complaining that *"...we have become insensitive to human life, to the wonders of this world, to the mystery within us and around us."* Merton's reply is one of the most eloquent dissertations on social activism, and the expectation of its success, to come out of the twentieth century.

After acknowledging Forest's despair and noting that Forest needs to accept it, Merton stuns his correspondent by advising him to *"not depend on the hope of results... You may have to face the fact that your work will be apparently worthless and even achieve no result at all, if not perhaps results opposite to what you expect. As you get used to this idea you start to concentrate more and more not on the results, but on the value, the rightness, the truth of the work itself. And there too a great deal has to be gone through, as gradually you struggle less and less for an idea and more and more for specific people... In the end... it is the reality of personal relationships that saves everything."*

---

[96] Havel, Václav. 1990.

From Emergency to Emergence Again

For some readers, if the last few paragraphs were not testing enough, then the coming paragraphs may be the most challenging reading in this book.

When we look through the eyes of a systems theorist at the world of today we can see that our current society is an emergent one. It has emerged from the interactions of millions of people over the past few hundred years. Can we lay the credit, or the blame, at the feet of any one of those people, or even at the feet of any group? No, says Margaret Wheatley, one of those systems theorists who has looked at the world and tried to understand how it works as a system and how it may change and adapt to new inputs to emerge into something different. In an article entitled *Absurd Heroism* she counsels us to not take too seriously our role in bringing this system about, nor to feel that it is all up to us to change it.

Wheatley recalls the myth of Sisyphus, who was condemned by the gods to continually roll a boulder to the top of a hill only for it to roll down again and for Sisyphus to begin the process all over again. Wheatley has this advice for activators: *"Sisyphus had no choice — he had been condemned by the gods. But we do have a choice. We can notice the price we're paying for our absurd heroism, for believing that it's up to us. I hear so many people who want to take at least partial responsibility for this mess. Somewhat piously, as if summoning us to accountability, they say, "We need to accept responsibility that we created this" or "We created it, so we can change it." No we didn't. And no we can't. We participated with innumerable other players and causes and this is what emerged. We can't take credit for it, we can't blame ourselves and we can't put the burden of change on us. We're not Sisyphus, condemned to a fate of absurd heroism."[97]*

Wheatley goes on to talk about using emergence, rather than fighting it. The system that has emerged (including all the

---

[97] Wheatley, Margaret.

emergencies mentioned at the beginning of this book) has also given rise to each and every one of us. We are all part of this system. What emergence tells us is that the best we can do is to form connections and networks. Within those networks, we work on discovering our shared humanity and our shared values. When we do this, emergence tells us that we will not know what the outcome will be. It is one of the paradoxes of emergence: we are both powerless and powerful at the same time. Once we realise that, we can step out of our ego and accept the flow of change.

But what does this COFFEE taste like?

To coffee aficionados all over the world, there are many qualities to look for in a good cup of coffee, but one of the most critical has to be taste. So, what does this **COFFEE** taste like? How can it be applied? Will it make a difference? Will we emerge from our state of multi-emergencies into the world we want?

Certainly, the thinking that this acronym provides you with allows you to engage in conversations at your kitchen table. The acronym can be applied in our community development, engagement or social justice work quite simply. Just as easily it allows us to enter into national and even international dialogues.

As we engage in all these conversations and dialogues we may find that the very act of encountering one another in encouraging ways creates the very opportunities that our world needs. Could it be that by seeking to change the world we are paddling against the current instead of letting the flow work for and with us? Could it be that by assessing the emergencies facing us as being external to us we miss the opportunities that exist in our present encounters? Tom Atlee, founder of the Co-Intelligence Institute, captures this idea succinctly when he writes that,[98] *"Our goal is no longer a desired state for society, but rather a desirable unfolding of society."*

What I am suggesting here is that the ideas contained within **COFFEE** may not be just a method by which we "solve" the multi-

---

[98] Atlee, Tom. 2003

emergencies facing us; it may contain some of the solutions themselves. Where Atlee uses the word *unfolding* I have used the word *emergence*, or in the terminology of the **COFFEE** acronym – Flow From.

This book began with the suggestion that in order to address the multi-emergency facing us we should look to emergence. Emergence is a challenging idea. It means giving up most of our cherished notions of who we are, what we want, how we get there, and who we get there with. Maybe, just maybe, however, it is exactly the new type of thinking and feeling that we need. It may be challenging, but as the **COFFEE** acronym suggests, it is, at heart, quite simple.

Now, how about that coffee!

Solution to Thinking Outside the Box puzzle (p 49)

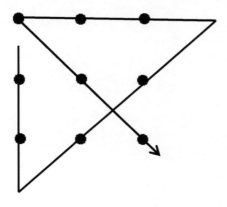

ACKNOWLEDGEMENTS

Over the years I have had hundreds (perhaps thousands) of cups of coffee with people, all of whom have helped mould my thinking and approach to how to change the world. I am indebted to all of them and hope that I managed to encourage them as much as they encouraged me.

When I think of this book, however, one name stands out as being the person who started it all. Deirdre Ryan was my team leader at Christchurch City Council until 2010. During our final one-on-one session, Deirdre said to me "Bruce, you should write." I took that as a compliment and not an assessment that I was no good at what I did and should go and write by myself somewhere. Thanks Deirdre, it was a wonderful encouragement. I hope that this book lives up to your expectations of me. To Michael McNabb, I enjoyed our many bohemian-philosophical breakfast discussions, and many of the topics we talked about can be found within these pages. A further Cantabrian that I wish to thank is Allison Franklin who did a superb job of proof-reading and editing my early manuscript.

In Coffs Harbour I have many people to thank for reading drafts and giving me feedback as I proceeded on the journey: Robin Macgregor, Lisa Siegal, Parul Punjabi, Ian Towner. Early encouragement from Peter Westoby from Queensland University allowed me to gain confidence that what I was writing had worth. I am grateful to Rosa Zubizarreta in the US, the more so because I have never met her, who offered encouragement on my last drafts. Thanks also to Elaine Ghali for suggesting the book's title.

I have suggested that the approach presented in this book is something new within western cultures. It is not so new to many indigenous cultures. My own thinking and experience has been greatly influenced by that of Māori culture in Aotearoa (New Zealand) and more recently by the Aboriginal culture of Australia. I acknowledge the ancestors and present elders of these cultures who have retained the link to ancient wisdom. Nga mihi mahana ki a koutou katoa – *Warm greetings to all of you.* I especially wish to thank Miriam-Rose Ungunmerr for allowing me to quote passages from *dadirri* on page 41 and page 111.

Thanks also to Glenn Anthony and the team at Dark Arts Coffee Academy in Coffs Harbour for helping get this project launched. To help me launch this I had the assistance of Elaine Sherwood and Julianne McKeon – thank you both so much.

I am graphically challenged so I am thankful for the artistic help of Rebecca Farr for designing the C.O.F.F.E.E. logo and to Charlieaja at Dreamstime for the stunning cover graphic.

Many people have commented on the text, the C.O.F.F.E.E. acronym, the cover design and other aspects of this book. For all of these comments and thoughts I am grateful. I'll try to name you all, but if I forget then please forgive me: Roger Meder, Lee Rickwood, Leonie Henschke, John Murray, David McRae, Gary Moller, Gary Norfolk, Jaqui Knowles, Kylie Castor, Stephanie Hunt.

Finally, but certainly not least, to Robyn Palmer I owe a cascade of roses for her support over years in which I had very limited income. Her help and friendship has been crucial.

ABOUT THE AUTHOR

Bruce Meder worked almost all his adult life in the fields of community development, community education and social justice. He has worked for the NZ Values Party (an early Green party), Friends Of the Earth (FOE), New Internationalist and many other community organisations.

He has helped edit and publish *Beyond Tomorrow* (NZ Values Party election manifesto) and *Peacelink* – a magazine devoted to the peace and indigenous rights movement in New Zealand and the Pacific.

Since the mid-1980s Bruce worked for national and local government. During that time he continued to work voluntarily with men's groups, environmental and peace groups in Christchurch. He also undertook lessons in Te Reo Māori (Māori language) inspired by a growing awareness of institutional and cultural racism in his country of birth.

The Christchurch earthquakes of 2010 and 2011 disrupted Bruce's life and he moved to Coffs Harbour in Australia where he has been involved with a men's mentoring group, the local climate action group and an Insight Meditation sangha. He obtains some employment as a facilitator with a restorative justice program.

Bruce spends much of his day researching and writing, and is a member of the Coffs Harbour Writers Group. He writes a weekly blog (rainbowjuice.org) dedicated to community development, social justice, and sustainability issues.

In his early life, Bruce worked as a gravedigger, coal bagger, postie, aircraft loader, part-time teacher, and land surveyor.

Bruce has a B.Sc. in mathematics, a Dip.Surv., and a Certificate in Continuing Education, but considers his own reading, research, and experience to have been the best education he has gained.

To find out more about Bruce and access his other writing visit www.brucemeder.com

BIBLIOGRAPHY

Atchley, RA, Strayer DL, Atchley P (2012) *Creativity in the Wild: Improving Creative Reasoning through Immersion in Natural Settings.* PLoS ONE 7(12): e51474. doi:10.1371/journal.pone.0051474.

Bandura, Albert: *The Psychology of Chance Encounters and Life Paths,* American Psychologist, Vol 37, No. 7, July 1982.

Born, Paul: *Community Conversations*, BPS Books, Toronto, 2008, 2012.

Brewer, Worhunsky, Gray, Tang, Weber & Kober: *Meditation experience is associated with differences in default mode network activity and connectivity,* Proceedings of the National Academy of Sciences (of the United States of America), 13 Dec 2011, Vol 108, No 50, pp 20254-20259.

Briskin, Erickson, Ott & Callanan: *The Power of Collective Wisdom and the trap of collective folly*, Berrett-Koehler Publishers, San Francisco, 2009.

Cain, Susan: *Quiet; The Power of Introverts in a World that Can't Stop Talking,* Crown Publishing Group, 2011.

Clements, Alan: *Instinct For Freedom; finding liberation through living,* Hodder, 2003.

Coover, Deacon, Esser & Moore: *Resource Manual for a Living Revolution*, New Society Press, Philadelphia, 1977.

Covey, Stephen R: *The 7 Habits of Highly Effective People*, Free Press, New York, 1989.

Csikszentmihalyi, Mihaly: *Flow: The Psychology of Optimal Experience*. Harper and Row, New York, 1990.

de Bono, Edward: *Serious Creativity*, Fontana, London, 1992.

Dunn, Claire: *My Year Without Matches*, Nero, Collingwood, Vic, Australia, 2014

Galinsky, Adam et al: *Power and perspectives not taken*, Psychological Science, 2006.

Galinsky, Adam et al: *Power and Overconfident decision making*, Organizational Behaviour and Human Decision Making Processes, March 2012.

GATT-Fly, *Ah-Hah: A new approach to popular education*. Between the Lines, Toronto, 1983, 1986.

Gerzon, Mark: *Leading Through Conflict*. Harvard Business School Press, Boston, 2006.

Goleman, Daniel: *Emotional Intelligence: why it can matter more than IQ,* Bloomsbury, London, 1996.

Havel, Václav: *Disturbing The Peace*, Vintage Books, New York, first English edition 1990.

Kidd, David & Castano, Emanuele: *Reading Literary Fiction Improves Theory of Mind*, in *Science* 18 Oct 2013: Vol. 342, Issue 6156, pp. 377-380.

Klein, Stefan: *Survival of the Nicest: how altruism made us human and why it pays to get along*, Scribe, London, 2014.

Knudtson, Peter & Suzuki, David: *Wisdom of the Elders*, Allen & Unwin, Toronto, 1992.

Krznaric, Roman: *The Empathy Effect How Empathy Drives Common Values, Social Justice and Environmental Action*, paper presented to Friends of the Earth, March 2015.

Lindahl, Kay: *Practicing the Sacred Art of Listening: a guide to enrich your relationship and kindle your spiritual life*, SkyLight Paths, Woodstock, VT. 2003.

Loh, Jonathan & Harmon, David: *Biocultural Diversity: Threatened species, endangered languages*, WWF-Netherlands, 2004.

Louv, Richard: *Last Child In The Woods: Saving our children from nature deficit disorder*, Workman Publishing Company, New York, 2005.

Loy, David: *Nonduality: A Study in Comparative Philosophy*, Humanity Books, New York, 1998.

Macy, Joanna & Brown, Molly: *Coming Back To Life*, New Society Publishers, Gabriola Island, BC, Canada, 2014.

Manz, Charles: *"The Power of Failure; 27 ways to turn life's setbacks into success"*: Berrett-Koehler Publishers, Oakland, 2009.

Meadows, Meadows, Randers & Behrens III: *Limits to Growth; a report for the Cub of Rome's project on the predicament of mankind*, Potomac Associates, Washington, 1972.

Meadows, Donella H.: *Thinking in Systems: A Primer,* Chelsea Green Publishing, White River Junction, Vermont, 2008.

Mrazek, Franklin, Phillips, Baird & Schooler: *Mindfulness Training Improves Working Memory Capacity and GRE Performance While Reducing Mind Wandering,* Psychological Science, May 2013, pp 776-781.

Plotkin, Bill: *Nature and the Human Soul,* New World Library, Novato, California, 2008.

Putnam, Robert: *Bowling Alone: The collapse and revival of American community,* Simon and Schuster, New York, 2000.

Senge, Scharmer, Jaworski, & Flowers: *Presence; exploring profound change in people, organizations and society,* Nicholas Brealey Publishing, London, 2005.

Smith, Rodney: *stepping out of self-deception: the buddha's liberating teaching of no-self,* Shambhala Publications, Boston, 2010.

Surowiecki, James: *The Wisdom of Crowds: Why the Many Are Smarter Than the Few and How Collective Wisdom Shapes Business, Economies, Societies and Nations,* Doubleday, New York, 2004.

Tutu, Desmond & Tutu, Mpho: *The Book of Forgiving,* William Collins, London, 2014.

Wehbe, Murphy, Talukdar, Fyshe, Ramdas, and Mitchell: *Simultaneously Uncovering the Patterns of Brain Regions Involved in Different Story Reading Subprocesses,* PLoS One. 2014; 9(11): e112575. Published online 2014 Nov 26.

Westoby, Peter & Dowling, Gerard: *Theory and Practice of Dialogical Community Development: International perspectives*, Routledge, London & New York, 2013.

Wheatley, Margaret: http://www.awakin.org/read/view.php?tid=2115

Zubizarreta, Rosa: *From Conflict to Creative Collaboration: A User's Guide to Dynamic Facilitation*, Two Harbors Press, Minneapolis, 2015.

INDEX

7 Habits of Highly Effective People, The (book), 85

A More Beautiful Question (book), 34

Aboriginal culture (Australia), 37, 58

activators: social, 29

adaptation, 10

adversity, 59; - opportunity from, 58, 59

African values, 60

agribusiness, 65

ah-hah seminar, 38

air: cycle of, 134

Allen, Woody, 46

Angelo, Natalia Gutierrez Y, 33

anxiety, 1, 3, 42, 70, 82, 108

apartheid, 60

apathy, 70

apocalypse, 4

Appreciative Inquiry, 121, 122

aquariums, 138

Arab Spring, 19, 20

Aristotle, 35

athletes, 70

Atlee, Tom, 160

Bakhtin: Mikhail, 132

Bandura, Albert, 113

Bannockburn (Battle of), 42

belief system, 79; cultural, 81

Berger, Warren, 34, 106

Better Days (song), 33

biodiversity, 65, 150

Bohm: David, 132

boredom, 70

Born, Paul, 119, 121

brainstorming, 29-31

breath, 134

Brontë sisters, 49

Buddhism, 81

Butterfly effect, 9, 18, 24, 113

C.O.F.F.E.E. aconym, 2, 11, 25, 53, 65, 70, 81, 95, 109, 141, 149, 151, 153, 154, 156, 160, 161

cause and effect, 7

Challenger (space shuttle), 67

Chaos Theory, vi, 1, 5, 68

Chaplin, Charlie, 107

Charlie Hebdo (French magazine), 100

Charrette, 122

choice-creating process. *See* facilitation - dynamic

Chronicles of Narnia, The (book), 123

citizens, 29, 75

Citizens' Councils. *See* Citizens juries

Citizens' juries, 117

Citizens' Panels. *See* Citizens' juries

Clements, Alan, 156

climate change, v, 1

Coast-to-Coast (mulitsport race),
   64
coffee, 2, 25, 26, 119, 149
Co-Intelligence Institute, 160
collaboration, 49
collective folly, 66, 67, 77, *See
   also collective wisdom*
collective wisdom, 66, 68, 77,
   116
Colombia: - Revolutionary
   Armed Forces of (FARC), 32
comfort zone, 62
Coming Back To Life (book), 136
communication, 12, 13, 15, 101,
   104; - non-verbal
   communication, 101;
   nonviolent. *See* nonviolent
   communication
community, vi, 10, 93
community development, v, vi, 5,
   10, 21, 55, 57, 60, 61, 66, 71;
   Asset Based Community
   Development, 55
compassion, 19, 146, 148
competition, 112
complexity, 1, 2, 7, 10, 11, 13, 15,
   24, 25, 69, 76, 78, 143, 149,
   156; Complexity Theory, 5
conflict, 60, 74, 102, 130;
   resolution, 133
conform: desire to, 49
connection, 40
consciousness, 40, 41, 51, 69, 70,
   81, 82, 100

consensus, 59, 67, 78, 114, 128
constellations, 140
consumers, vi, 15, 28
consumption, 150
control, 64, 65; desire for, 65, 66,
   71; need to.., 40
Copernicus, 35
corruption, 65
Covey, Stephen, 85, 89
creativity, 27-53, 69, 70, 83, 85,
   86, 89, 105, 106, 110, 134;
   collective, 48, 53
Crosby, Ned, 118
Csikszentmihalyi, Mihaly, 68, 70
cultural bias, 137
culture, 37, 80; healthy or
   unhealthy, 145
culture - iceberg model of, 80
Curie, Marie, 49
curiosity, 34, 35, 71, 89
da Vinci, Leonardo, 49
dadirri, 37, 110, See also inner
   listening
Dalai Lama, 146
Darwin, Charles, 111, 137
de Bono, Edward, 31, 48, 49; six
   thinking hats, 31
decision-making, vii, 4, 73, 74,
   78, 109, *114*, 129
democracy, 4, 19, 20, 60, 61
depression, 1, 3, 82, 108
Descartes: Rene, 143
Descent of Man, The (book), 111
development, 73

dialogue, 77, 78, 130, 132
Diaz, Alfonso, 33
diversity, 8, 29, 36, 49, 56, 57, 149, 150
domestic violence, vi
Down and Out in Paris and London (book), 90, 92
Doyle, Kevin, 78
dreams, 28; daydreaming, 40
Dunn, Claire, 141
Dyer, Dr Wayne, 40
dynamic facilitation, 129
ecocentricism, 136, 144, 146
eco-psychology, 135, 137
eco-systems, 8, 111, 151
Edison, Thomas, 42, 43, 49
ego, 100
ego-centricism, 145
einfühling (empathy), 86
Einstein, Albert, 8, 27, 34, 45, 49, 50, 79, 146
Eisenberg, Nancy, 86
emergence, 1, 5, 15, 17- 20, 24, 63, 151, 159, 160, 161
emergencies, 1, 2, 4, 5, 29, 36, 48, 49, 51, 56, 65, 66, 78, 143, 147, 161
emotions, 39, 87, 88, 91, 104
empathy, 85, 87, 88, 89, 91, 92, 146
emptiness, 81
encounters, 26, 45, 70, 71, 112, 113; chance, 113

encouragement, 67, 85, 93, 106, 107, 147
encouraging, 26, 49, 63, 70, 83, 94, 97, 99, 101, 102, 103, 106, 107, 108, 109, 110
end justifies the means, 65
Enlightenment, 7
Espejo, Colonel Jose, 32, 34
experts, 29, 73-76
extinction of species, 150
extroversion, 49, 104, 105
Facebook, 12, 19
facilitation, 114, 124; dynamic, 128-130
failure, 42- 44; - fear of, 42-43
feedback, 10, 106
feelings, 32, 39, 44, 86, 87, 88, 94, 102, 103, 104, 105, 107; - feeling wheel, 88
financial systems, 14
fix-it mentality, 153
flow, 63-71, 73, 110; chaotic, 65
Flowers, Betty Sue, 52
food, 108, 109
Forest, Jim, 158
freedom of speech, 61, 100
Freire, Paulo, 39
from, 26
Future Search, 116
Galileo, 35
Gallegos, Eligio, 41
Galton, Francis, 76
Gandhi, Mohatma, 49
gardening, 139

GATT-Fly, 38, 39
Gaza Strip, 3
Gerzon, Mark, 130
globalisation, 15, 150
goat in the well (story), 58
government, 4
group dynamics: 114, group
    needs and personal needs, 126
Great North West Youth Summit,
    22, 24
great turning, the, 136
Gropius, Walter, 75
Havel, Václav, 158
heart, 41, 51, 136; -centred
    thinking, 51
Hector's Dolphins, 133
heliocentric system, 79
hiking (tramping, trekking), 139
Hobbit, The (book), 123
honesty, 94
humour, 107; - affiliative, 107
ideology, 60, 61, 62, 155
imagination, 28, 29, 40, 41, 50,
    90
improvisation, 46
indigenous culture, 37, 56, 59,
    109
Industrial Revolution, 135
inequality, 65
information, 13; overload, 14
Inklings, The, 123
innovation: technological, 50
instinct, 41
interbeing, 144

introversion, 49, 97, 104, 105
intuition, 28, 32, 38, 39, 40, 41,
    146
Jaworski, Joseph, 52
Je Suis Charlie, 100
Jefferson Center, 118
Jordan, Michael, 42, 43
judgment, 83, 85, 103;
    suspending, 102
Kennedy, J F, 79
Kenyon, Peter, 55
knowledge, 36, 56, 57, 73; - edge
    of, 36; collective, 73; common,
    76
Krznaric, Roman, 89, 92
Lao Tzu, 125
lateral thinking, 31, 34, 45, 48
law of two feet, 120
Le Corbusier, 75
left-brain, right-brain, 27, 28
Lehrer, James, 50
leverage points, 155
Lewis, C S, 123
Limits to Growth, The (book), 154
Lindahl, Kay, 100
listening: 37, 44, 48, 66, 83, 85,
    94, 101, 103, 109, 128,-
    creative, 95, 99, 129, 147; -
    creative listening techniques,
    96 -97 - inner listening, 37
Lord of the Rings (book), 123
Lorenz, Edward, 8
Louv, Richard, 135
Loy, David, 81

Lyell, Charles, 112
Macleans (Canadian magazine), 78
Macy, Joanna, 65, 136, 147
Madson, Patricia Ryan, 46
Mandela, Nelson, 60, 61
Manz, Charles, 43, 44
Māori (indigenous people of Aoteraroa - New Zealand), 108
Meadows, Donella, 154, 155
meditation, 82, 83, 147; benefits of, 82; walking, 140
Mega, Voula, 44
men, 57, 87
Merton, Thomas, 158
mirror neurons, 86
moccasins (walk a mile in), 90
Monet, Claude, 49
monkey mind, 82
Morse code, 33
movies, 92
NASA, 67
nature, 137, 145, *170*; - wandering in, 137; disconnection from, 138; encountering, 133, 136, 141, 146; humans as part of, 53
nature deficit disorder, 135
Nature Principle, The (book), 136
neuroplasticity, 87
neuroscience, 86, 146
Newton, Issac, 49, 50
Newton's Laws, 5
non-action. *See* wu wei

nonviolent communication (NVC), 103, 104
Nuremberg Trials, 61
occupy movement, 20
old lady and the fly (children's ditty), 52
Open Space (Unconference), 118, 119, 121
opportunities, *43*, 47, 55-62, 63, 65, 83; missed, 60, 61
order, 17
Origin of Species (book), 111
Ortiz, Juan Carlos, 32, 33
Orwell: George, 90, 92
Owen, Harrison, 119
paradigms, vi, 155
patterns, 40, 49
People's Verdict, 78
perfectionism, 42
PhotoVoice, 123
Pietzker, Mary Ann, 99
Playback Theatre, 46
Plotkin, Bill, 135, 136, 137, 146
politicians, 4, 57, 61, 65, 73
power, 4, 65, 73, 74
Power of Collective Wisdom (book), 67
prejudice, 73, 74, 83
present (being), 64, 71, 85, 95, 101, 102, 105
problem-solving, 52, 109, 129; mind-set, 52
Putnam, Robert, 93
Quakers, 114

quantum physics, 8

questioning, 34, 35, 36, 40, 53, 106

questions, vi, 29, 36, 106; open and closed, 106

Radio Bemba (Colombian recording studio), 33

reading, 91, 92

reliability, 94

Resource Manual for a Living Revolution (book), 114

restorative justice, 58

Ridington, Robin, 57

Robb, Kaitlin, 88

Robert the Bruce, 42, 43

Robert's Rules of Order, 114, 124

Rogers, Carl, 103

Ronan Point (tower block), 75

Rosenberg, Marshall, 103

Rough, Jim, 129

Scharmer, Otto, 52

self 141-148: alienation from our sense of, 53; as emergent phenomenon, 142; centred, 71; conscious, 71; healthy, 145; separate, 143; unhealthy, 145

self-organising (principle), 136, 137, 156

Senge, Peter, 52

sensitivity to initial conditions, 10

Serious Creativity (book), 48

shift the burden (trap of), 53

shunyata, 81

silence, 96, 97, 105

Simon, Herbert A, 38

simplicity, 11

Sisyphus (myth of), 159

skills development, 98

social capital, 93

social change, 25, 57, 89, 92

social engineering, 113

social justice, 5, 66, 71

speaking, 99

spirit, 100

spontaneity, 18, 19, 20

spooky action, 8

Strayer, Janet, 86

success, 42, 43, 44

Surowiecki, James, 77

survival of the fittest, 111, 137

sustainability, 5, 20, 66

sympathy, 85, 86

systems thinking, 153, 155, 159

T.H.I.N.K. acronym, 99, 100

Tahrir Square, 19

tall poppy syndrome, 44

Taoism, 68

Te Koru Pou Iho (Papanui Youth Facility), 24

technology, 13, 15

television, 93

The Power of Failure (book), 43

Thich Nhat Hanh, 144

tiger walking, 139

time, 109, 110

Toffler, Alvin, 14

Tolkien, J R R, 123

transnationals, 65

travel, 12
trust, 85, 93, 94
trust walk (exercise), 140
Truth and Reconciliation
    Commission (South Africa), 61
Tutu: Bishop Desmond, 61, 144
Twain, Mark, 47
ubuntu, 144
Umbrella Revolution (Hong
    Kong), 44
unconference. *See* open space
Ungunmeer: Miriam-Rose, 37,
    146
unpredictability, 1, 17, 20, 156
waste, 137
water: cycle, 134
waterfalls, 140
Wheatley, Margaret, 159, 160
Whose Line Is It Anyway? (TV
    show), 46
Wilberforce, William, 35
wilderness, 134, 137, 141
wisdom, 29, 39, 53, 56, 57, 73,
    74, 75; collective, 53
wisdom of crowds, 76, *See* also
    collective wisdom
Wollstonecraft, Mary, 49
women, 57
work that reconnects, 136
World Café, 115
World Wide Opportunities on
    Organic Farms (WWOOF),
    141

World Wildlife Fund (WWF),
    150
World-View: Western, 5
wu wei, 68
youth, 21, 22, 23; youth suicide,
    1, 3
Zangger, Heinrich (friend of
    Albert Einstein), 51
Zappa, Frank, 66
zoos, 138
Zulu, 144

179

If you found the C.O.F.F.E.E. acronym useful, then here are some products that will help you remember it and to let others know of it.

Men's and Women's Organic Cotton T-shirts

A range of mugs, plus other items. All available at

www.brucemeder.com

Printed in Great Britain
by Amazon